THE LITTLE BOOK

of

COMMON SENSE
INVESTING

10th Anniversary Edition | Updated & Revised

Little Book Big Profits Series

In the *Little Book Big Profits* series, the brightest icons in the financial world write on topics that range from tried-and-true investment strategies to tomorrow's new trends. Each book offers a unique perspective on investing, allowing the reader to pick and choose from the very best in investment advice today.

Books in the *Little Book Big Profits* series include:

Books by John C. Bogle

1994 *Bogle on Mutual Funds: New Perspectives for the Intelligent Investor*
—Foreword by Paul A. Samuelson

1999 *Common Sense on Mutual Funds: New Imperatives for the Intelligent Investor*
—Foreword by Peter L. Bernstein

2001 *John Bogle on Investing: The First 50 Years*
—Foreword by Paul A. Volcker, Introduction by Chancellor William T. Allen

2002 *Character Counts: The Creation and Building of the Vanguard Group*

2005 *The Battle for the Soul of Capitalism*
—Foreword by Peter G. Peterson

2007 *The Little Book of Common Sense Investing: The Only Way to Guarantee Your Fair Share of Stock Market Returns*

2008 *Enough. True Measures of Money, Business, and Life*
—Foreword by William Jefferson Clinton, Prologue by Tom Peters

2010 *Common Sense on Mutual Funds: Fully Updated 10th Anniversary Edition*
—Foreword by David F. Swensen

THE LITTLE BOOK

of

COMMON SENSE INVESTING

The Only Way to Guarantee
Your Fair Share of Stock Market Returns

10th Anniversary Edition | Updated & Revised

JOHN C. BOGLE

WILEY

To the memory of the late Paul A. Samuelson,
professor of economics
at Massachusetts Institute of Technology,
Nobel Laureate, investment sage.
In 1948 when I was a student at Princeton
University, his classic textbook introduced me
to economics. In 1974, his writings reignited my
interest in market indexing as an investment strategy.
In 1976, his *Newsweek* column applauded my creation
of the world's first index mutual fund. In
1993, he wrote the foreword to my first book, and
in 1999 he provided a powerful endorsement for my
second. While he departed this life in 2009, he remains
my mentor, my inspiration, my shining light.

Contents

Chapter Twenty
Investment Advice That Meets the
Test of Time

Introduction to the 10th Anniversary Edition

———— ∾ ————

Don't Allow a Winner's Game to Become a Loser's Game.

SUCCESSFUL INVESTING IS ALL about common sense. As Warren Buffett, the Oracle of Omaha, has said, it is simple, but it is not easy. Simple arithmetic suggests, and history confirms, that the winning strategy for investing in stocks is to own all of the nation's publicly held businesses at very low cost. By doing so you are guaranteed to capture almost the entire return that these businesses generate in the form of dividends and earnings growth.

The best way to implement this strategy is indeed simple: *Buy a fund that holds this all-market portfolio, and hold it forever*. Such a fund is called an index fund. The index fund is simply a basket (portfolio) that holds many, many eggs (stocks) designed to mimic the overall performance of the U.S. stock market (or any financial market or market sector).[1] The traditional index fund (TIF), by definition, basically represents the entire stock market basket, not just a few scattered eggs. It eliminates the risk of picking individual stocks, the risk of emphasizing certain market sectors, and the risk of manager selection. Only stock market risk remains. (That risk is quite large enough, thank you!) Index funds make up for their lack of short-term excitement by their truly exciting long-term productivity. The TIF is designed to be held for a lifetime.

~

The index fund eliminates the risks of individual stocks, market sectors, and manager selection. Only stock market risk remains.

This is much more than a book about index funds. It is a book that is determined to change the very way that you

---

[1] Keep in mind that an index may also be constructed around the bond market, or even "road less traveled" asset classes such as commodities or real estate. Today, if you wish, you could literally hold all your wealth in a diversified portfolio of low-cost traditional index funds representing every asset class and every market sector within the United States or around the globe.

think about investing. It is a book about why long-term investing serves you far better than short-term speculation; about the value of diversification; about the powerful role of investment costs; about the perils of relying on a fund's past performance and ignoring the principle of *reversion (or regression) to the mean* (RTM) in investing; and about how financial markets work.

When you understand how our financial markets actually work, you will see that the index fund is indeed the only investment that essentially guarantees that you will capture your fair share of the returns that business earns. Thanks to the miracle of compounding, the accumulations of wealth that are generated by those returns over the years have been little short of fantastic.

The traditional index fund (TIF).

I'm speaking here about the traditional index fund. The TIF is broadly diversified, holding all (or almost all) of its share of the $26 trillion capitalization of the U.S. stock market in early 2017. It operates with minimal expenses and with no advisory fees, with tiny portfolio turnover, and with high tax efficiency. That traditional index fund—the first one tracked the returns of the

Standard & Poor's 500 Index—simply owns shares of the dominant firms in corporate America, buying an interest in each stock in the stock market in proportion to its market capitalization, and then holding it forever.

～

The magic of compounding investment returns.
The tyranny of compounding investment costs.

Please don't underestimate the power of compounding the generous returns earned by our businesses. Let's assume that the stocks of our corporations earn a return of 7 percent per year. Compounded at that rate over a decade, each $1.00 initially invested grows to $2.00; over two decades, to $4.00; over three decades, to $7.50; over four decades, to $15.00, and over five decades, to $30.00.[2]

The magic of compounding is little short of a miracle. Simply put, thanks to the growth, productivity, resourcefulness, and innovation of our corporations, capitalism

---

[2] Over the past century, the average nominal return on U.S. stocks was 10.1 percent per year. In real terms (after 3.4 percent inflation) the *real* annual return was 6.7 percent. During the next decade, both returns are likely to be significantly lower. (See Chapter 9.)

creates wealth, a *positive-sum game for its owners. Investing in equities for the long term has been a winner's game.*

The returns earned by business are ultimately translated into the returns earned by the stock market. I have no way of knowing what share of these market returns you have earned in the past. But academic studies suggest that if you are a typical investor in individual stocks, your returns have probably lagged the market by around two percentage points per year.

Applying that figure to the annual return of 9.1 percent earned over the past 25 years by the Standard & Poor's 500 Stock Index, your annual return has likely been in the range of 7 percent. Result: investors as a group have been served only about three-quarters of the market pie. In addition, as explained in Chapter 7, if you are a typical investor in mutual funds, you've done even worse.

——————— ∾ ———————

A zero-sum game?

If you don't believe that return represents what most investors experience, please think for a moment about "the relentless rules of humble arithmetic" (Chapter 4). These iron rules define the game. As investors, all of us as a group earn the stock market's return.

As a group—I hope you're sitting down for this astonishing revelation—we investors are average. For each percentage point of extra return above the market that one of us earns, another of our fellow investors suffers a return shortfall of precisely the same dimension. *Before the deduction of the costs of investing, beating the stock market is a zero-sum game.*

A loser's game.

As investors seek to outpace their peers, winners' gains inevitably equal losers' losses. With all that feverish trading activity, the only sure winner in the costly competition for outperformance is the person who sits in the middle of our financial system. As Warren Buffett recently wrote, "When trillions of dollars are managed by Wall Streeters charging high fees, it will usually be the managers who reap outsize profits, not the clients."

In the casino, the house always wins. In horse racing, the track always wins. In the Powerball lottery, the state always wins. Investing is no different. In the game of investing, the financial croupiers always win, and investors as a group lose. *After the deduction of the costs of investing, beating the stock market is a loser's game.*

**Less to Wall Street croupiers means more to Main
Street investors.**

Successful investing, then, is about minimizing the
share of the returns earned by our corporations that is consumed by Wall Street, and maximizing the share of returns
that is delivered to Main Street. (That's *you*, dear reader.)

Your chances of earning your fair share of the market's returns are greatly enhanced if you minimize your
trading in stocks. One academic study showed that during the strong bull market of 1990–1996 the most active
one-fifth of all stock traders turned their portfolios over at
the rate of more than 21 percent per month. While they
earned the annual market return of 17.9 percent during
that bull market period, they incurred trading costs of
about 6.5 percent, leaving them with an annual return of
but 11.4 percent, only two-thirds of the market return.

Mutual fund investors, too, have inflated ideas of their
own omniscience. They pick funds based on the recent
performance superiority—or even the long-term superiority—of a fund manager, and often hire advisers to help
them achieve the same goal (Warren Buffett's "Helpers,"
described in the next chapter). But as I explain in Chapter
12, the advisers do it with even less success.

Oblivious of the toll taken by costs, too many fund investors willingly pay heavy sales loads and incur excessive fund fees and expenses, and are unknowingly subjected to the substantial but undisclosed transaction costs incurred by funds as a result of their hyperactive portfolio turnover. Fund investors are confident that they can consistently select superior fund managers. *They are wrong.*

Mutual fund investors are confident that they can easily select superior fund managers. *They are wrong.*

Contrarily, for those who invest and then drop out of the game and never pay a single unnecessary cost, the odds in favor of success are awesome. Why? Simply because they own shares of *businesses*, and businesses as a group earn substantial returns on their capital, pay out dividends to their owners, and reinvest what's left for their future growth.

Yes, many individual companies fail. Firms with flawed ideas and rigid strategies and weak managements ultimately fall victim to the *creative destruction* that is the hallmark of competitive capitalism, only to be succeeded by other firms.[3] But in the aggregate, businesses have grown with the long-term growth of our vibrant economy. Since 1929, for example, our nation's gross domestic product (GDP) has grown at a nominal annual rate of 6.2 percent; annual pretax profits of our nation's corporations have grown at a rate of 6.3 percent. The correlation between the growth of GDP and the growth of corporate profits is 0.98. (1.0 is perfect.) I assume that this long-term relationship will prevail in the years ahead.

Get out of the casino and stay out!

This book intends to show you why you should stop contributing to the croupiers of the financial markets. Why? Because during the past decade they have raked in something like $565 billion each year from you and your fellow investors. It will also tell you how easy it is to avoid those croupiers: Simply buy a Standard & Poor's 500 Index fund or a total stock market index fund. Then, once you have bought your stocks, get out of the casino—and stay out. Just hold the market portfolio forever. And that's what the traditional index fund does.

---

[3] "Creative destruction" is the formulation of Joseph E. Schumpeter in his 1942 book *Capitalism, Socialism, and Democracy*.

Simple but not easy.

This investment philosophy is not only simple and elegant. The arithmetic on which it is based is irrefutable. But it is not easy to follow its discipline. So long as we investors accept the status quo of today's crazy-quilt financial market system, so long as we enjoy the excitement (however costly) of buying and selling stocks, and so long as we fail to realize that there is a better way, such a philosophy will seem counterintuitive. But I ask you to carefully consider the impassioned message of this *Little Book*. When you do, you too will want to join the index revolution and invest in a new, "more economical, more efficient, even more honest way,"[4] a more productive way that will put your own interests first.

Thomas Paine and *Common Sense*.

It may seem farfetched for me to hope that any single book could ignite the spark of a revolution in investing.

---

[4] "Economical," "efficient," and "honest" are the words I used in my 1951 Princeton University thesis, "The Economic Role of the Investment Company." Some principles are eternal.

New ideas that fly in the face of the conventional wisdom of the day are always greeted with doubt and scorn, even fear. Indeed, 240 years ago, the same challenge was faced by Thomas Paine, whose 1776 tract *Common Sense* helped spark the American Revolution. Here is what Tom Paine wrote:

> Perhaps the sentiments contained in the following pages are not yet sufficiently fashionable to procure them general favor; a long habit of not thinking a thing wrong, gives it a superficial appearance of being right, and raises at first a formidable outcry in defense of custom. But the tumult soon subsides. Time makes more converts than reason. . . . I offer nothing more than simple facts, plain arguments, and common sense.

As we now know, Thomas Paine's powerful and articulate arguments carried the day. The American Revolution led to our Constitution, which to this day defines the responsibilities of our government and our citizens, the very fabric of our society.

Similarly, I believe that in the coming era, my own simple facts, plain arguments, and common sense will carry the day for investors. The Index Revolution will help us build a new and more efficient investment system for our nation, a system in which serving investors is its highest priority.

Structure and strategy.

Some may suggest that, as the creator both of Vanguard in 1974 and of the world's first index mutual fund in 1975, I have a vested interest in persuading you of my views. *Of course I do!* But not because it enriches me. It doesn't earn me a penny. Rather, I want to persuade you because those two rocks on which Vanguard was founded all those years ago—our truly mutual, fund-shareholder-owned structure and our index fund strategy—will enrich *you* over the long term.

Don't take my word for it!

In the early years of indexing, my voice was a lonely one. But there were a few other thoughtful and respected believers whose ideas inspired me to carry on my mission. Today, many of our wisest and most successful investors endorse the index fund concept; among academics, the acceptance is close to universal. *But don't take my word for it.* Listen to these independent experts who have no ax to grind except for the truth about investing. You'll hear from some of them at the end of each chapter.

Listen, for example, to this endorsement by the late Paul A. Samuelson, Nobel laureate in economic sciences and professor of economics at the Massachusetts Institute of Technology, to whose memory this book is dedicated: "Bogle's reasoned precepts can enable a few million of us savers to become in twenty years the envy of our suburban neighbors—while at the same time we have slept well in these eventful times."

It will take a long time to fix our financial system. But the glacial pace of that change should not prevent you from looking after your own self-interest. You don't need to participate in its expensive foolishness. If you choose to play the winner's game of owning shares of businesses, and to refrain from playing the loser's game of trying to beat the market, you can begin the task simply by using your own common sense, understanding the system, and eliminating substantially all of its excessive costs.

Then, at last, you will be guaranteed to earn your fair share of whatever returns our businesses may be generous enough to deliver in the years ahead, reflected as they will be in our stock and bond markets. (Caution: You'll also earn your fair share of any interim negative returns.) When you understand these realities, you'll see that it's all about common sense.

---------------- ⌇ ----------------

The 10th Anniversary Edition of *The Little Book of Common Sense Investing.*

When the first edition of *The Little Book of Common Sense Investing* was published 10 years ago, my hope was that investors would find it useful in helping them to earn their fair share of whatever returns—positive or negative—our financial markets deliver.

That original *Little Book* of 2007 was a direct successor to my first book, *Bogle on Mutual Funds: New Perspectives for the Intelligent Investor*, published in 1994. Both books set forth the case for index investing, and both became the best-selling mutual fund books ever, with investors purchasing a combined total of more than 500,000 copies.

During the near quarter-century since the publication of my first book, index funds have come into their own. Assets of equity index funds have risen 168-fold, from $28 billion to $4.6 trillion in mid-2017. In the past decade alone, U.S. investors have added $2.1 trillion to their holdings of equity index funds and withdrawn more than $900 billion from their holdings of actively managed equity funds. Such a huge $3 trillion swing in investor preferences surely represents no less than an investment revolution.

In retrospect, it seems clear that my pioneering creation of the first index mutual fund in 1975 provided the spark that ignited the index revolution. And it also seems reasonable to conclude that my books, read by an estimated 1.5 million readers, played a major role in fueling the extraordinary power of the revolution that followed.

The creative destruction reaped by index funds has, by and large, served investors well. As you read this 10th Anniversary Edition of *The Little Book of Common Sense Investing*, you'll see that it stands firmly behind the sound principles of its predecessors, with new chapters on dividends, asset allocation, and retirement planning focused on the implementation of those principles.

Learn! Enjoy! Act!

JOHN C. BOGLE

Valley Forge, Pennsylvania
September 1, 2017

Don't Take My Word for It

Charles T. Munger, Warren Buffett's business partner at Berkshire Hathaway, puts it this way: "The general systems of money management [today] require people to pretend to do something they can't do and like something they don't.

(continued)

[It's] a funny business because on a net basis, the whole investment management business together gives no value added to all buyers combined. *That's the way it has to work.* Mutual funds charge 2 percent per year and then brokers switch people between funds, costing another three to four percentage points. The poor guy in the general public is getting a terrible product from the professionals. I think it's disgusting. It's much better to be part of a system that delivers value to the people who buy the product."

* * *

William Bernstein, investment adviser (and neurologist), and author of *The Four Pillars of Investing,* says: "It's bad enough that you have to take market risk. Only a fool takes on the additional risk of doing yet more damage by failing to diversify properly with his or her nest egg. Avoid the problem—buy a well-run index fund and own the whole market."

* * *

Here's how the *Economist* of London puts it: "The truth is that, for the most part, fund managers have offered extremely poor value for money.

Their records of outperformance are almost always followed by stretches of underperformance. Over long periods of time, hardly any fund managers have beaten the market averages.... And all the while they charge their clients big fees for the privilege of losing their money.... [One] specific lesson ... is the merits of indexed investing ... you will almost never find a fund manager who can repeatedly beat the market. It is better to invest in an indexed fund that promises a market return but with significantly lower fees."

* * *

It's really amazing that so many giants of academia, and many of the world's greatest investors, known for beating the market, confirm and applaud the virtues of index investing. May their common sense, perhaps even more than my own, make you all wiser investors.

NOTE: *Little Book* readers interested in reviewing the sources for the "Don't Take My Word for It" quotes found at the end of each chapter, other quotes in the main text, and the sources of the extensive data that I present can find them on my website: www.johncbogle.com. I wouldn't dream of consuming valuable pages in this small book with a weighty bibliography, so please don't hesitate to visit my website.

Chapter One

A Parable

~

The Gotrocks Family

Even before you think about "index funds"—in their most basic form, mutual funds that simply buy shares of substantially all of the stocks in the U.S. stock market and hold them forever—you must understand how the stock market actually works. Perhaps this folksy parable—my version of a story told by Warren Buffett, chairman of Berkshire Hathaway, Inc., in the firm's 2005 Annual Report—will clarify the foolishness and counterproductivity of our vast and complex financial market system.

Once upon a Time . . .

A wealthy family named the Gotrocks, grown over the generations to include thousands of brothers, sisters, aunts, uncles, and cousins, owned 100 percent of every stock in the United States. Each year, they reaped the rewards of investing: all of the earnings growth that those thousands of corporations generated and all of the dividends that they distributed.[1] Each family member grew wealthier at the same pace, and all was harmonious. Their investment compounded over the decades, creating enormous wealth. The Gotrocks family was playing a winner's game.

But after a while, a few fast-talking Helpers arrive on the scene, and they persuade some "smart" Gotrocks cousins that they can earn a larger share than their relatives. These Helpers convince the cousins to sell their shares in some of the companies to other family members, and to buy shares of other companies from them in return. The Helpers handle the transactions and, as brokers, they receive commissions for their services. The ownership is thus rearranged among the family members. To their surprise, however, the family wealth begins to grow at a slower pace. Why? Because some of the investment return is now consumed by the Helpers, and the family's share of the generous pie

---

[1] To complicate matters just a bit, the Gotrocks family also purchased the new public offerings of securities that were issued each year.

that U.S. industry bakes each year—all of those dividends paid, all those earnings reinvested in the businesses—100 percent at the outset, starts to decline, simply because some of the return is now consumed by the Helpers.

To make matters worse, in addition to the taxes the family has always paid on their dividends, some of the members are now also paying capital gains taxes. Their stock-swapping back and forth generates capital gains taxes, further diminishing the family's total wealth.

The smart cousins quickly realize that their plan has actually diminished the rate of growth in the family's wealth. They recognize that their foray into stock-picking has been a failure, and conclude that they need professional assistance, the better to pick the right stocks for themselves. So they hire stock-picking experts—more Helpers!—to gain an advantage. These money managers charge fees for their services. So when the family appraises its wealth a year later, it finds that its share of the pie has diminished even further.

To make matters still worse, the new managers feel compelled to earn their keep by trading the family's stocks at feverish levels of activity, not only increasing the brokerage commissions paid to the first set of Helpers, but running up the tax bill as well. Now the family's earlier 100 percent share of the dividends and earnings pie is further diminished.

"Well, we failed to pick good stocks for ourselves, and when that didn't work, we also failed to pick managers who could do so," the smart cousins say. "What shall we do?" Undeterred by their two previous failures, they decide to hire still more Helpers. They retain the best investment consultants and financial planners that they can find to advise them on how to select the right managers, who will then surely pick the right stocks. The consultants, of course, tell them that they can do the job. "Just pay us a fee for our services," the new Helpers assure the cousins, "and all will be well." Alas, with those added costs, the family's share of the pie tumbles once again.

Get rid of all your Helpers. Then your family will again reap 100 percent of the pie that corporate America bakes for you.

Alarmed at last, the family sits down together and takes stock of the events that have transpired since some of them began to try to outsmart the others. "How is it," they ask, "that our original 100 percent share of the pie—made up each year of all those dividends and earnings—has dwindled to just 60 percent?" Their wisest member, a sage old uncle, softly responds: "All that money you've paid to those Helpers and all those unnecessary extra taxes you're paying come directly out of our family's total earnings and dividends. *Go back to square one, and do so immediately. Get rid of all your brokers. Get rid of all your money managers. Get rid of all your consultants.* Then our family will again reap 100 percent of however large a pie corporate America bakes for us, year after year."

They followed the old uncle's wise advice, returning to their original passive but productive strategy, holding all the stocks of corporate America, and standing pat.

That is exactly what an index fund does.

. . . and the Gotrocks Family Lived Happily Ever After

Adding a fourth law to Sir Isaac Newton's three laws of motion, the inimitable Warren Buffett puts the moral of his story this way: For investors as a whole, returns decrease as motion increases.

Accurate as that cryptic statement is, I would add that the parable reflects the profound conflict of interest between those who work in the investment business and those who invest in stocks and bonds. The way to wealth for those in the business is to persuade their clients, *"Don't just stand there. Do something."* But the way to wealth for their clients in the aggregate is to follow the opposite maxim: *"Don't do something. Just stand there."* For that is the only way to avoid playing the loser's game of trying to beat the market.

When a business is conducted in a way that directly defies the interests of its clients in the aggregate, it is only a matter of time until the clients awaken to reality. Then, the change comes—and that change is driving the revolution in our financial system today.

The moral of the Gotrocks story: Successful investing is about owning businesses and reaping the huge rewards provided by the dividends and earnings growth of our nation's—and, for that matter, the world's—corporations. *The higher the level of their investment activity, the greater the cost of financial intermediation and taxes, the less the net return that shareholders—as a group, the owners of our businesses—receive.* The lower the costs that investors as a group incur, the higher the rewards that they reap. So to enjoy the winning returns generated by businesses over the long term, the intelligent investor will reduce to the barebones minimum the costs of financial intermediation. That's what common sense tells us. That's what indexing is all about. And that's the central message of this book.

Don't Take My Word for It

Listen to **Jack R. Meyer**, former president of Harvard Management Company, the remarkably successful wizard who tripled the Harvard University endowment fund from $8 billion to $27 billion. Here's what he had to say in a 2004 *BusinessWeek* interview: "*The investment business is a giant scam.* Most people think they can find managers who can outperform, but most people are wrong. I will say that 85 to 90 percent of managers fail to match their benchmarks. Because managers have fees and incur transaction costs, you know that in the aggregate they are deleting value."

When asked if private investors can draw any lessons from what Harvard does, Mr. Meyer responded, "Yes. First, get diversified. Come up with a portfolio that covers a lot of asset classes. Second, you want to keep your fees low. That means avoiding the most hyped but expensive funds, in favor of low-cost index funds. And finally, invest for the long term. [Investors] should simply have index funds to keep their fees low and their taxes down. *No doubt about it.*"

* * *

In terms that are a bit less contentious, Princeton University professor **Burton G. Malkiel**, author of *A Random Walk Down Wall Street*, expresses these views: "Index funds have regularly

(continued)

produced [annual] rates of return exceeding those of active managers by close to 2 percentage points. Active management as a whole cannot achieve gross returns exceeding the market as a whole, and therefore they must, on average, underperform the indexes by the amount of these expense and transaction costs.

"Experience conclusively shows that index-fund buyers are likely to obtain results exceeding those of the typical fund manager, whose large advisory fees and substantial portfolio turnover tend to reduce investment yields. . . . The index fund is a sensible, serviceable method for obtaining the market's rate of return with absolutely no effort and minimal expense."

Chapter Two

Rational Exuberance

*Shareholder Gains Must Match
Business Gains.*

Tʜᴀᴛ ᴡᴏɴᴅᴇʀꜰᴜʟ ᴘᴀʀᴀʙʟᴇ ᴀʙᴏᴜᴛ the Gotrocks family in Chapter 1 brings home the central reality of investing: "The most that owners in aggregate can earn between now and Judgment Day is what their businesses in aggregate earn," in the words of Warren Buffett. Illustrating the point with Berkshire Hathaway, the publicly owned corporation that he has run for 46 years, please heed carefully Mr. Buffett's statement:

> When the stock temporarily overperforms or underperforms the business, a limited number of shareholders—either sellers or buyers—receive outsized benefits at

the expense of those they trade with. . . . Over time, the aggregate gains made by Berkshire shareholders must of necessity match the business gains of the company.

⁓

"Over time, the aggregate gains made by . . . shareholders must of necessity match the business gains of the company."

How often investors lose sight of that eternal principle! Yet the record is clear. History, if only we would take the trouble to examine it, reveals the remarkable, if essential, linkage between the cumulative long-term returns earned by U.S. business—the annual dividend yield plus the annual rate of earnings growth—and the cumulative returns earned by the stock market. Think about that certainty for a moment. Can you see that it is simple common sense?

Need proof? Just look at the record since the beginning of the twentieth century (Exhibit 2.1). The average annual total return on stocks was 9.5 percent. The *investment* return alone was 9.0 percent—4.4 percent from dividend yield and 4.6 percent from earnings growth.

That difference of 0.5 percentage points per year arose from what I call *speculative* return. Speculative return may be a plus or a minus, depending on the willingness

**EXHIBIT 2.1   Investment Return versus Market Return.
Growth of $1, 1900–2016**

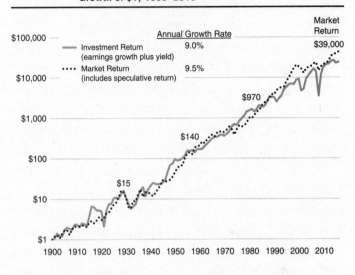

of investors to pay either higher or lower prices for each dollar of earnings at the end of a given period than at the beginning.

The price/earnings (P/E) ratio measures the number of dollars investors are willing to pay for each dollar of earnings. As investor confidence waxes and wanes, P/E multiples rise and fall.[1] When greed holds sway, very high P/Es are likely. When hope prevails, P/Es are moderate. When fear is in the saddle, P/Es are typically very low.

---

[1] Changes in interest rates also have an impact, uneven though it may be, on the P/E multiple. So, I'm oversimplifying a bit here.

Back and forth, over and over again, swings in the emotions of investors are reflected in speculative return. They momentarily derail the steady long-range upward trend in the economics of investing.

As reflected in Exhibit 2.1, the investment return on stocks—dividend yield plus earnings growth—tracks closely with the total market return (including the impact of speculative return) over the long term. Any significant divergences between the two are short-lived.

Compounding these returns over 116 years produces accumulations that are truly staggering. Each dollar initially invested in stocks in 1900 at a return of 9.5 percent grew by the close of 2015 to $43,650.[2] Sure, few (if any) of us have 116 years in us! But our descendants follow us, and, like the Gotrocks family, enjoy the miracle of compounding returns. These returns have been little short of amazing—the ultimate winner's game.

As Exhibit 2.1 makes clear, there are bumps along the way in the investment returns earned by our business corporations. Sometimes, as in the Great Depression of the early 1930s, these bumps were large. But we got over

---

[2] But let's be fair. If we compound that initial $1, not at the *nominal* return of 9.5 percent but at the *real* rate of 6.3 percent (after 3.2 percent inflation during the period), $1 grows to $1,339, but a fraction of the accumulation in nominal terms. But increasing real wealth more than 1,300 times over is not to be sneezed at.

them. So, if you stand back from the chart and squint your eyes, the trend of business fundamentals looks almost like a straight line sloping gently upward, and those periodic bumps are barely visible.

Reversion to the mean.

To be sure, stock market returns sometimes get well ahead of business fundamentals (as in the late 1920s, the early 1970s, and the late 1990s, perhaps even today). But it has been only a matter of time until, as if drawn by a magnet, they ultimately return to the long-term norm, although often only after falling well behind for a time, as in the mid-1940s, the late 1970s, and the 2003 market lows. It's called reversion (or regression) to the mean (RTM), which we'll discuss in depth in Chapter 11.

In our foolish focus on the short-term stock market distractions of the moment, we investors often overlook this long history. When the returns on stocks depart materially from the long-term norm, we ignore the reality that it is rarely because of the *economics* of investing—the earnings growth and dividend yields of our corporations. Rather, the reason that annual stock returns are so volatile is largely because of the *emotions* of investing, reflected in those changing P/E ratios.

———————— ∾ ————————

"It is dangerous . . . to apply to the future inductive arguments based on past experience."

What Exhibit 2.1 shows is that while the prices we pay for stocks often lose touch with the reality of corporate values, *in the long run reality rules*. So, while investors seem to intuitively accept that the past is inevitably prologue to the future, any past stock market returns that have included a high speculative stock return component are deeply flawed guides to what lies ahead. To understand why past returns do not foretell the future, we need only heed the words of the great British economist John Maynard Keynes. Here's what he wrote 81 years ago:

> It is dangerous . . . to apply to the future inductive arguments based on past experience, unless one can distinguish the broad reasons why past experience was what it was.

But if we *can* distinguish the reasons the past was what it was, then we can establish reasonable expectations about the future. Keynes helped us make this distinction by pointing out that the state of long-term expectation for stocks is a combination of enterprise ("forecasting the prospective yield of assets over their whole life") and speculation ("forecasting the psychology of the market").

I'm well familiar with those words, for 66 years ago I incorporated them into my senior thesis at Princeton University. It was entitled, "The Economic Role of the Investment Company." It led, providentially, to my lifetime career in the mutual fund industry.

~

The dual nature of stock market returns.

This dual nature of returns is clearly reflected when we look at stock market returns over the decades (Exhibit 2.2). Putting my own numbers to Keynes's idea, I divide stock market returns into two parts: (1) *investment return* (enterprise), consisting of the initial dividend yield on stocks plus their subsequent earnings growth (together, they form the essence of what we call "intrinsic value"), and (2) *speculative return*, the impact of changing price/earnings multiples on stock prices. Let's begin with investment returns.

The top section of Exhibit 2.2 shows the average annual investment return on stocks over each of the decades since 1900. Note first the steady contribution of dividend yields to total return during each decade: always positive, only twice outside the range of 3 percent to 7 percent, and averaging 4 percent.

**EXHIBIT 2.2   Total Stock Returns by the Decade, 1900–2016
(Percent Annually)**

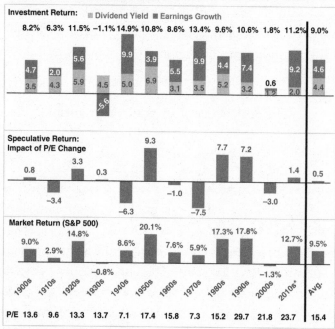

* Through 2016. P/Es at the end of each decade are noted above. The 1900 P/E was 12.5.

Then note that the contribution of earnings growth
to investment return, with the exception of the depres-
sion-ridden 1930s, was positive in every decade and above
9 percent in several decades, but usually ran between
4 percent and 7 percent, and averaged 4.6 percent per year.

Result: Total investment returns (the top section, combining dividend yield and earnings growth) were negative in only a single decade (again, in the 1930s). While these decade-long total investment returns—the gains made by business—varied, I consider them remarkably steady. They generally ran in the range of 8 percent to 13 percent annually, and averaged 9 percent.

Enter speculative return.

Enter speculative return, shown in the middle section of Exhibit 2.2. Compared with the relative consistency of dividends and earnings growth over the decades, truly wild variations in speculative return punctuate the chart. P/Es wax and wane, often with a remarkable impact on returns. For example, a 100 percent rise in the P/E, from 10 to 20 times over a decade, would equate to a 7.2 percent annual speculative return.

As you can see, without exception *every* decade of significantly negative speculative return was immediately followed by a decade in which it turned positive by a correlative amount: the negative 1910s and then the roaring 1920s; the dispiriting 1940s and then the booming 1950s; the discouraging 1970s and then the soaring 1980s.

This pattern is reversion to the mean writ large. RTM can be thought of as the tendency for those P/Es to return to their long-term norms over time. Periods of subpar performance tend to be followed by periods of recovery, and vice versa. Then, amazingly, during the 1990s, there was an unprecedented second consecutive exuberant increase, a pattern never before in evidence.

A return to sanity.

In April 1999, the P/E ratio had risen to an unprecedented level of 34 times, setting the stage for the return to sanity in valuations that soon followed. The tumble in stock market prices gave us our comeuppance. With earnings continuing to rise, the P/E currently stands at 23.7 times, compared with the 15 times level that prevailed at the start of the twentieth century. As a result, speculative return has added just 0.5 percentage points to the annual investment return earned by our businesses over the long term.[3]

---

[3] Our measure of the P/E ratio at the close of 2016 is based on the year-end price of 2247 for the S&P 500 relative to *reported earnings* for 2016 of $95 per share—a P/E of 23.7. Wall Street analysts tend to rely on *operating earnings* (before write-offs and other negatives) that are forecast for the coming year ($118 per share). Resulting P/E: 17.4 times.

Combining investment return and speculative return: total stock market returns.

When we combine these two sources of stock returns, we get the total return produced by the stock market. (The lower section of Exhibit 2.2.) Despite the huge impact of speculative return—up *and* down—during most of the individual decades, there is virtually *no* impact over the long term. The average annual total return on stocks of 9.5 percent, then, has been created almost entirely by *enterprise*, with only 0.5 percentage point created by *speculation*.

The message is clear: In the long run, stock returns depend almost entirely on the reality of the investment returns earned by our corporations. The perception of investors, reflected by the speculative returns, counts for little. It is economics that controls long-term equity returns; the impact of emotions, so dominant in the short term, dissolves.

Accurately forecasting short-term swings in investor emotions is not possible. But forecasting the long-term economics of investing has carried remarkably high odds of success.

Even after more than 66 years in this business, I have almost no idea how to forecast these short-term swings in investor emotions.[4] But, largely because the arithmetic of investing is so basic, I have been able to forecast the long-term economics of investing with remarkably high odds of success.

Why? Simply because it is *investment* returns—the earnings and dividends generated by American businesses—that are almost entirely responsible for the returns delivered in our stock market over the long term. While illusion (the momentary prices we pay for stocks) often loses touch with reality (the intrinsic values of our corporations), it is reality that rules in the long run.

--------------------------- ∽ ---------------------------

The real market and the expectations market.

To drive this point home, think of investing as consisting of two different games. Here's how Roger Martin, dean of the Rotman School of Management of the University of Toronto, describes them. One game is "the *real* market, where giant publicly held companies compete. Where real

---

[4] I'm not alone. I don't know anyone who has done so consistently, nor even anyone who knows anyone who has done so. In fact, 70 years of financial research finds no one who has done so.

companies spend real money to make and sell real products and services, and, if they play with skill, earn real profits and pay real dividends. This game also requires real strategy, determination, and expertise; real innovation and real foresight." Loosely linked to this game is another game, the *expectations* market. Here, "prices are not set by real things like sales margins or profits. In the short term, stock prices go up only when the expectations of investors rise, not necessarily when sales, margins, or profits rise."

The stock market is a giant distraction to the business of investing.

To this crucial distinction, I would add that the expectations market is largely a product of the expectations of *speculators*, trying to guess what other investors will expect and how they will act as each new bit of information finds its way into the marketplace. *The expectations market is about speculation. The real market is about investing. The stock market, then, is a giant distraction to the business of investing.*

Too often, the market causes investors to focus on transitory and volatile short-term expectations, rather than on what is really important—the gradual accumulation of the returns earned by corporate businesses.

When Shakespeare wrote that "it is a tale told by an idiot, full of sound and fury, signifying nothing," he could have been describing the inexplicable daily, month-by-month, or even annual swings in stock prices. My advice to investors: ignore the short-term sound and fury of the emotions reflected in our financial markets, and focus on the productive long-term economics of our corporate businesses. The way to investment success is to get out of the expectations market of stock prices and cast your lot with the real market of business.

Don't Take My Word for It

Simply heed the timeless distinction made by **Benjamin Graham**, legendary investor, author of *The Intelligent Investor*, and mentor to Warren Buffett. He was right on the money when he put his finger on the essential reality of investing: *"In the short run the stock market is a voting machine . . . in the long run it is a weighing machine."*

Using his wonderful metaphor of "Mr. Market," Ben Graham says, "Imagine that in some private business you own a small share which cost you $1,000. One of your partners, named Mr. Market, is very obliging indeed. Every day he tells you what

---

he thinks your interest is worth and furthermore offers either to buy you out or to sell you an additional interest on that basis. Sometimes his idea of value appears plausible and justified by business developments and prospects as you know them. Often, on the other hand, Mr. Market lets his enthusiasm or his fears run away with him, and the value he proposes seems little short of silly.

"If you are a prudent investor . . . will you let Mr. Market's daily communication determine your view as the value of your $1,000 interest in the enterprise? Only in case you agree with him, or in case you want to trade with him. . . . But the rest of the time you will be wiser to form your own ideas of the value of your holdings. . . . The true investor . . . will do better *if he forgets about the stock market and pays attention to his dividend returns and to the operating results of his companies.* (Italics added.) . . .

"The investor with a portfolio of sound stocks should expect their prices to fluctuate and should neither be concerned by sizable declines nor become excited by sizable advances. He should always remember that market quotations are there for his convenience, either to be taken advantage of or to be ignored."

Chapter Three

Cast Your Lot with Business

Win by Keeping It Simple—Rely on Occam's Razor.

How do you cast your lot with business? Simply by buying a portfolio that owns shares of every business in the United States and then holding it forever. This simple concept guarantees you will win the investment game played by most other investors who—as a group—are guaranteed to lose.

Please don't equate simplicity with stupidity. Way back in 1320, William of Occam nicely expressed the virtue of simplicity, essentially setting forth this precept:

When there are multiple solutions to a problem, choose the simplest one.[1] And so *Occam's razor* came to represent a major principle of scientific inquiry. By far the simplest way to own all of U.S. businesses is to hold the total stock market portfolio or its equivalent.

Occam's razor: When there are multiple solutions to a problem, choose the simplest one.

For the past 90 years, the accepted stock market portfolio has been represented by the Standard & Poor's 500 Index (the S&P 500). It was created in 1926 as the Composite Index, and now lists 500 stocks.[2] It is essentially composed of the 500 largest U.S. corporations, weighted by the value of their market capitalizations. In recent years, these 500 stocks have represented about 85 percent of the market value of all U.S. stocks. The beauty of such a *market-cap-weighted* index is that it never needs to be rebalanced by buying and selling shares due to changing stock prices.

---

[1] William of Occam expressed it more elegantly: "Entities should not be multiplied unnecessarily." But the point is unmistakable.
[2] Until 1957, the S&P Index included just 90 companies.

With the enormous growth of corporate pension funds between 1950 and 1990, the S&P 500 was an ideal measurement standard, the benchmark (or *hurdle rate*) that would be the comparative standard for how the professional managers of pension funds were performing. Today, the S&P 500 remains a valid standard against which to compare the returns earned by the professional managers of pension funds and mutual funds.

The Total Stock Market Index

In 1970, an even more comprehensive measure of the U.S. stock market was developed. Originally called the Wilshire 5000, it is now named the Dow Jones Wilshire Total Stock Market Index.[3] It now includes some 3,599 stocks, including the 500 stocks in the S&P 500. Because its component stocks also are weighted by their market capitalization, those remaining 3,099 stocks with smaller capitalizations account for only about 15 percent of its value.

---

[3] Full disclosure: Vanguard created the first index mutual fund, tracking the Standard & Poor's 500 Index, in 1975. The firm also created the first Total Stock Market Index Fund in 1992.

This broadest of all U.S. stock indexes is the best measure of the aggregate value of stocks, and therefore a superb measure of the returns earned in U.S. stocks by all investors as a group. As just indicated, both indexes hold the very same large stocks. Exhibit 3.1 shows the 10 largest stocks in each, and their weights in the construction of each index.

EXHIBIT 3.1   S&P 500 versus Total Stock Market Index: Portfolio Comparison, December 2016

S&P 500		Total Stock Market Index	
Rank	Weighting	Rank	Weighting
Apple Inc.	3.2%	Apple Inc.	2.5%
Microsoft Corp.	2.5	Microsoft Corp.	2.0
Alphabet Inc.	2.4	Alphabet Inc.	2.0
Exxon Mobil Corp.	1.9	Exxon Mobil Corp.	1.6
Johnson & Johnson	1.6	Johnson & Johnson	1.3
Berkshire Hathaway Inc.	1.6	Berkshire Hathaway Inc.	1.3
JPMorgan Chase & Co.	1.6	JPMorgan Chase & Co.	1.3
Amazon.com Inc.	1.5	Amazon.com Inc.	1.3
General Electric Co.	1.4	General Electric Co.	1.2
Facebook Inc.	1.4	Facebook Inc.	1.1
Top 10	19.1%	Top 10	15.6%
Top 25	33.3	Top 25	27.3
Top 100	63.9	Top 100	52.9
Top 500	100.0	Top 500	84.1
Total market cap	$19.3 trillion		$22.7 trillion

Given the similarity of these two portfolios, it is hardly surprising that the two indexes have earned returns that are in lockstep with one another. The Center for Research in Security Prices at the University of Chicago has gone back to 1926 and calculated the returns earned by all U.S. stocks. The returns of the S&P 500 Index and the Dow Jones Wilshire Total Stock Market Index parallel one another with near precision. From 1926, the beginning of the measurement period, through 2016, you can hardly tell them apart (Exhibit 3.2).

For the full period, the average annual return on the S&P 500 was 10.0 percent; the return on the Total Stock

EXHIBIT 3.2   S&P 500 and Total Stock Market Index, 1926–2016

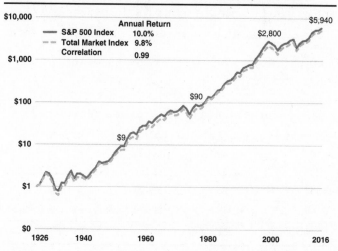

Market Index was 9.8 percent. This comparison is what we call *period dependent*—everything depends on the starting date and the ending date. If we were to begin the comparison at the beginning of 1930 instead of 1926, the returns of the two would be identical: 9.6 percent per year.

Yes, there are variations over the interim periods: the S&P 500 was much the stronger from 1982 to 1990, when its annual return of 15.6 percent outpaced the Total Stock Market Index return of 14.0 percent. But since then, small- and mid-cap stocks have done a bit better, and the Total Stock Market Index return of 10.2 percent per year narrowly exceeded the 9.9 percent return of the S&P 500. But with a long-term correlation of 0.99 between the returns of the two indexes (1.00 is perfect correlation), there is little to choose between the two.[4]

~

Returns earned in the stock market must equal the gross returns earned by all investors in the market.

---

[4] You should know that, in establishing a trust for his wife's estate, Warren Buffett directed that 90 percent of its assets be invested in a low-cost S&P 500 Index fund.

Whichever measure we use, it should now be obvious that the returns earned by the publicly held corporations that compose the stock market must of necessity equal the aggregate gross returns earned by all investors in that market as a group. Equally obvious, as will be discussed in Chapter 4, the net returns earned by these investors must of necessity fall short of those aggregate gross returns by the amount of intermediation costs they incur. Our common sense tells us the obvious, just what we learned in Chapter 1: *Owning the stock market over the long term is a winner's game, but attempting to* beat *the stock market is a loser's game.*

A low-cost all-market fund, then, is guaranteed to outpace over time the returns earned by equity investors as a group. Once you recognize this fact, you can see that the index fund is guaranteed to win not only over time, but every year, and every month and week, even every minute of the day. No matter how long or short the time frame, the gross return in the stock market, minus intermediation costs, equals the net return earned by investors as a group. If the data do not prove that indexing wins, well, the data are wrong.

∼

If the data do not prove that indexing wins, well, the data are wrong.

Over the short term, however, it doesn't always look as if the S&P 500 (still the most common basis of comparison for mutual funds and pension plans) or the Total Stock Market Index is winning. That is because there is no possible way to calculate precisely the returns earned by the millions of diverse participants, amateur and professional alike, Americans and foreign investors, in the U.S. stock market.

In the mutual fund field, we calculate the returns of the various funds, counting each fund—regardless of the amount of its assets—as a single entry. Since there are many small-cap and mid-cap funds, usually with relatively modest asset bases, at times they may have a disproportionate impact on the data. When small- and mid-cap funds are leading the total market, the all-market index fund seems to lag. When small- and mid-cap stocks are lagging the market, the index fund looks formidable indeed.

Active funds versus benchmark indexes.

The obvious solution to the challenge of comparing active equity funds of all types with the S&P 500 Index is to measure funds against other indexes that more closely reflect their own investment strategies. Some years ago, the

S&P Indices versus Active (SPIVA) report began to do exactly that. The report provides comprehensive data comparing active mutual funds grouped by various strategies with relevant market indexes. In its 2016 year-end report, SPIVA extended the longest time horizon evaluated in the report to 15 years (2001–2016) and reported the percentage of actively managed funds that were outperformed by their relevant benchmark indexes. The results were impressive (Exhibit 3.3). On average, an astonishing 90 percent of actively managed mutual funds underperformed their benchmark indexes over the preceding 15 years. The index superiority was consistent and overwhelming.

The S&P 500 outpaced 97 percent of actively managed large-cap core funds. The S&P 500 Growth and Value indexes are used as comparisons for funds in those large-cap categories, and so on for the three mid-cap categories and the three small-cap categories. The sweeping across-the-board superiority of the indexes can leave little doubt that index funds are here to stay.

EXHIBIT 3.3   Percentages of Actively Managed Mutual Funds Outperformed by Comparable S&P Indexes, 2001–2016

Fund Category	Growth	Core	Value
Large-Cap	95%	97%	79%
Mid-Cap	97	99	90
Small-Cap	99	95	81

In 1951, I wrote in my senior thesis at Princeton University that mutual funds "can make no claim to superiority over the market averages." Sixty-six years later, that has proven to be a huge understatement.

— ∿ —

The record of an investor in the first index mutual fund: $15,000 invested in 1976; value in 2016, $913,340.

The recent era not only has failed to erode, but has nicely enhanced the lifetime record of the world's first index fund—now known as the Vanguard 500 Index Fund. It began operations back on August 31, 1976. Let me be specific: at a luncheon on September 20, 2016, celebrating the 40th anniversary of the fund's initial public offering, the counsel for the fund's underwriters reported that he had purchased 1,000 shares at the original offering price of $15 per share—a $15,000 investment. He proudly announced the value of his holding that day (including shares acquired through reinvesting the fund's dividends and distributions over the years in additional shares): $913,340.[5] Now, there's a number that requires no embellishment. But it does demand one caveat and one caution.

---

[5] This investor paid separately the taxes due on dividends and capital gains distributions.

~

A caveat and a caution.

The caveat: Of the 360 equity mutual funds in existence when the first index fund was formed in 1976, only 74 remain. Actively managed funds come and go, but the index fund goes on forever. *The caution*: During that four-decade period, the S&P 500 Index grew at an annual rate of 10.9 percent. With today's lower dividend yields, the prospect of lower earnings growth, and aggressive market valuations, it would be foolish in the extreme to assume that such a return would recur over the next four decades. See Chapter 9, "When the Good Times No Longer Roll."

The past record confirms that owning American business through a broadly diversified index fund is not only logical but, to say the least, incredibly productive. Equally important, it is consistent with the age-old principle of simplicity expressed by Sir William of Occam: Instead of joining the crowd of investors who dabble in complex algorithms or other machinations to pick stocks, or who look to past performance to select mutual funds, or who try to outguess the stock market (for investors in the aggregate, three inevitably fruitless tasks), choose the simplest of all solutions—buy and hold a diversified, low-cost portfolio that tracks the stock market.

Don't Take My Word for It

Hear **David Swensen,** the widely respected chief investment officer of the Yale University Endowment Fund. "[Over the fifteen years ending 1998, a] minuscule 4 percent of [mutual] funds produced market-beating after-tax results with a scant 0.6 percent [annual] margin of gain. The 96 percent of funds that fail to meet or beat the Vanguard 500 Index Fund lose by a wealth-destroying margin of 4.8 percent per annum."

* * *

The simple index fund solution is used not only by investors of average means. It has been adopted as a cornerstone of investment strategy for many of the nation's pension plans operated by our giant corporations and state and local governments. Indexing is also the predominant strategy for the largest plan of them all, the retirement plan for federal government employees, the federal Thrift Savings Plan (TSP). The plan now holds some $460 billion of assets for the benefit of our public servants and members of our armed services. All contributions and earnings are tax-deferred until withdrawal, much like the corporate 401(k) thrift plan.[6]

* * *

Indexing is also praised across the Atlantic "pond." Listen to these words from **Jonathan Davis**, columnist for London's *The Spectator*: "Nothing highlights better the continuing gap between rhetoric and substance in British financial services than the failure of providers here to emulate Jack Bogle's index fund success in the United States. Every professional in the City knows that index funds should be core building blocks in any long-term investor's portfolio. Since 1976, the Vanguard index fund has produced a compound annual return of 12 percent, better than three-quarters of its peer group. Yet even 30 years on, ignorance and professional omerta still stand in the way of more investors enjoying the fruits of this unsung hero of the investment world."

---

[6] The TSP also offers Roth contributions, which are treated similarly to Roth IRAs for tax purposes. Roth contributions are made with after-tax income, but all subsequent growth is completely tax free. I'll expand on the subject of saving for retirement in Chapter 19.

Chapter Four

How Most Investors Turn a Winner's Game into a Loser's Game

---

*"The Relentless Rules of
Humble Arithmetic"*

BEFORE WE TURN TO the success of indexing as an investment strategy, let's explore in a bit more depth just why it is that investors as a group fail to earn the returns that our corporations generate through their dividends and earnings growth, which are ultimately reflected in the prices of their stocks. Why? Because investors as a group must necessarily earn precisely the market return, *before the costs of investing are deducted.*

When we subtract those costs of financial intermediation—all those management fees, all of that portfolio turnover, all of those brokerage commissions, all of those sales loads, all of those advertising costs, all of those operating costs, all of those legal fees—the returns of investors as a group must, and will, and do fall short of the market return by an amount precisely equal to the aggregate amount of those costs. *That is the simple, undeniable reality of investing.*

In a market that returns 7 percent in a given year, we investors together earn a gross return of 7 percent. (Duh!) But after we pay our financial intermediaries, we pocket only what remains. (And we pay them whether our returns are positive or negative!)

∽

Before costs, beating the market is a zero-sum game. After costs, it is a loser's game.

There are, then, these two certainties: (1) *Beating the market before costs is a zero-sum game.* (2) *Beating the market after costs is a loser's game.* The returns earned by investors in the aggregate inevitably fall well short of the returns that are realized in our financial markets. How much do those costs come to? For individual investors

holding stocks directly, trading costs may average 1.5 percent or more per year. That cost is lower (maybe 1 percent)
for those who trade infrequently, and much higher for
investors who trade frequently (for example, 3 percent for
investors who turn their portfolios over at a rate above
200 percent per year).

In actively managed equity mutual funds, management fees and operating expenses—combined in what we
call a fund's *expense ratio*—average about 1.3 percent per
year, and about 0.8 percent when weighted by fund assets.
Then add, say, another 0.5 percent in sales charges, assuming that a 5 percent initial sales charge were spread over
a 10-year holding period. If the shares were held for five
years, the sales charge cost would be twice that 0.5 percent
figure—1 percent per year. (Many funds carry sales loads,
now often spread over a decade or more. About 60 percent
of funds are "no-load" funds.)

But then add a giant additional cost, all the more
pernicious by being invisible. I am referring to the hidden costs of portfolio turnover, which I estimate average
a full 1 percent per year. Actively managed mutual funds
are said to turn their portfolios over at a rate of about
80 percent per year, meaning, for example, that a $5 billion
fund buys $2 billion of stocks each year and sells another
$2 billion, a total of $4 billion. At that volume, brokerage

commissions, bid-ask spreads, and market impact costs add a major layer of additional costs that are borne by fund investors, perhaps 0.5 to 1.0 percent.

We investors as a group get precisely what we *don't* pay for. If we pay nothing, we get everything.

Result: the "all-in" cost of equity fund ownership can come to as much as 2 percent to 3 percent per year.[1] So yes, *costs matter*. The grim irony of investing, then, is that we investors as a group not only don't get what we pay for. We get precisely what we *don't* pay for. *So if we pay nothing, we get everything*. It's only common sense.

A few years ago when I was rereading *Other People's Money*, by Louis D. Brandeis (first published in 1914), I came across a wonderful passage that illustrates this simple lesson. Brandeis, later to become one of the most influential jurists in the history of the U.S. Supreme Court, railed against the oligarchs who a century ago controlled investment America and corporate America alike.

---

[1] I've ignored the hidden opportunity cost that fund investors pay. Most equity funds hold about 5 percent in cash reserves. If stocks earn a return of 7 percent and these reserves earn 2 percent, that cost would add another 0.25 percentage points to the annual cost (5 percent of assets multiplied by the 5 percent differential in earnings).

───────────── ∽ ─────────────

"The relentless rules of humble arithmetic."

───────────────────────────────

Brandeis described their self-serving financial management and their interlocking interests as *"trampling with impunity on laws human and divine, obsessed with the delusion that two plus two make five."* He predicted (accurately, as it turned out) that the widespread speculation of that era would collapse, *"a victim of the relentless rules of humble arithmetic."* He then added this unattributed warning (I'm guessing it's from Sophocles): *"Remember, O Stranger, arithmetic is the first of the sciences, and the mother of safety."*

Brandeis's words hit me like the proverbial ton of bricks. Why? Because the relentless rules of the arithmetic of investing are so obvious. (It's been said by my detractors that all I have going for me is "the uncanny ability to recognize the obvious.")

The curious fact is that most investors seem to have difficulty recognizing what lies in plain sight, right before their eyes. Or, perhaps even more pervasively, they refuse to recognize the reality because it flies in the face of their deep-seated beliefs, biases, overconfidence, and uncritical acceptance of the way that financial markets have worked, seemingly forever.

---------------------------- ∿ ----------------------------

It's amazing how difficult it is for a man to understand something if he's paid a small fortune *not* to understand it.

What's more, it is hardly in the interest of our financial intermediaries to encourage their investor/clients to recognize the obvious reality. Indeed, the self-interest of the leaders of our financial system almost compels them to ignore these relentless rules. Paraphrasing Upton Sinclair: *It's amazing how difficult it is for a man to understand something if he's paid a small fortune* not *to understand it.*

Our system of financial intermediation has created enormous fortunes for those who manage other people's money. Their self-interest will not soon change. But as an investor, you must look after *your* self-interest. Only by facing the obvious realities of investing can an intelligent investor succeed.

How much do the costs of financial intermediation matter? Hugely! In fact, the high costs of equity funds have played a determinative role in explaining why fund managers have lagged the returns of the stock market so consistently, for so long. When you think about it, how could it be otherwise?

By and large, these managers are smart, well-educated, experienced, knowledgeable, and honest. *But they are competing with one another.* When one buys a stock, another sells it. There is no net gain to fund shareholders as a group. In fact, they incur a loss equal to the transaction costs they pay to those "Helpers" that Warren Buffett warned us about in Chapter 1.

Investors pay far too little attention to the costs of investing. It's especially easy to underrate their importance under today's three conditions: (1) when stock market returns have been high (since 1980, stock returns have averaged 11.5 percent per year, and the average fund has provided a nontrivial—but clearly inadequate—return of 10.1 percent); (2) when investors focus on short-term returns, ignoring the truly confiscatory impact of costs over an investment lifetime; and (3) when so many costs are hidden from view (portfolio transaction costs, the largely unrecognized impact of front-end sales changes, and taxes incurred on fund distributions from capital gains, often realized unnecessarily).

Perhaps an example will help. Let's assume that the stock market generates a total return averaging 7 percent per year over a half century. Yes, that may seem a long time. But an investment lifetime is now actually even longer than that—65 or 70 years for an investor who goes to work at age 22; begins to invest immediately and works until, say, age 65; and then continues to invest over an actuarial life expectancy of 20 or more years thereafter. Now let's assume that the average mutual fund operated at a cost of at least an assumed 2 percent per year. Result: a *net* annual return of just 5 percent for the average fund.

$10,000 grows to $294,600 . . . or to $114,700. Where did that $179,900 go?

Based on these assumptions, let's look at the returns earned on $10,000 over 50 years (Exhibit 4.1). Assuming a nominal annual return of 7 percent, the simple investment in the stock market grows to $294,600. Why? The magic of compounding *returns* over an investment lifetime. In the early years, the line showing the growth at a 5 percent annual rate doesn't look all that different from the growth in the stock market itself.

But, ever so slowly, the lines begin to diverge, finally resulting in a truly dramatic gap. By the end of the 50-year period, the value accumulated in the fund totals just $114,700, an astounding shortfall of $179,900 to the cumulative return earned in the market itself. Why? The tyranny of compounding *costs* over that lifetime.

EXHIBIT 4.1   The Magic of Compounding Returns, the Tyranny of Compounding Costs: Growth of $10,000 over 50 Years

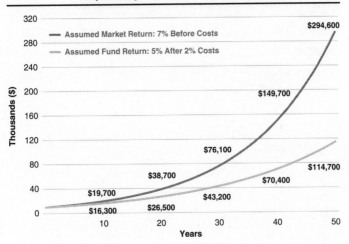

In the investment field, time doesn't heal all wounds. It makes them worse. *Where returns are concerned, time is your friend. But where costs are concerned, time is your enemy.* This point is powerfully illustrated when we consider how much of the value of the $10,000 investment is eroded with each passing year (Exhibit 4.2).

By the end of the first year, only about 2 percent of the potential value of your capital has vanished ($10,700 vs. $10,500). By the 10th year, 17 percent has vanished ($19,700 vs. $16,300). By the 30th year, 43 percent has vanished ($76,100 vs. $43,200). And by the end of the

EXHIBIT 4.2   The Tyranny of Compounding: Long-Term Impact of Lagging the Market by 2 Percent

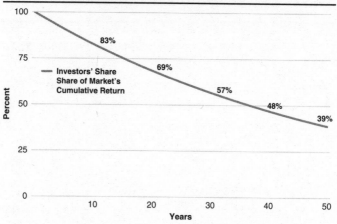

50-year investment period, costs have consumed 61 percent of the potential accumulation available simply by holding the market portfolio, leaving only 39% for the investor.

> You put up 100 percent of the capital and you assume 100 percent of the risk. But you earn less than 40 percent of the potential return.

In this example, the investor, who put up 100 percent of the capital and assumed 100 percent of the risk, earned less than 40 percent of the potential market return. Our system of financial intermediation, which put up zero percent of the capital and assumed zero percent of the risk, essentially confiscated 60 percent of that return.

I repeat: What you see in this example—and please don't ever forget it!—is that over the long term, the miracle of compounding *returns* has been overwhelmed by the tyranny of compounding *costs*. Add that mathematical certainty to the relentless rules of humble arithmetic described earlier.

Simply put, our fund managers, sitting at the top of the investment food chain, have confiscated an excessive share of the returns delivered by our financial markets. Fund investors, inevitably at the bottom of the food chain, have been left with a shockingly small share. Investors need not have incurred that loss, for they could have easily invested in a simple, very low-cost index fund tracking the S&P 500.

~

Costs make the difference between investment success and investment failure.

In short, the humble arithmetic of investing—the logical, inevitable, and unyielding penalty assessed by investment costs—has devastated the returns earned by mutual fund investors. Using Justice Brandeis's formulation, our mutual fund marketers seem *"obsessed with the delusion"* that investors capture 100 percent of the stock market's return—and are foisting that delusion on investors.

When our fund marketers cite the stock market's historical annual return of 9.5 percent since 1900 and ignore fund expenses of 2 percent and inflation of 3 percent, they suggest that investors can expect a real, after-cost return of 9.5 percent. Well, to state the obvious, they shouldn't. You need only add and subtract for yourself. The truth is that the real return to investors equals (you guessed it!) only 4.5 percent.

Fund investors deserve a fair shake.

Unless the fund industry gives its investors a fair shake and improves the net return that it delivers to fund shareholders, it will falter and finally fail—a victim, yes, of the relentless rules of humble arithmetic. Were he looking over your shoulder as you read this book, Justice Brandeis surely would be warning you, *"Remember, O reader, that arithmetic is the first of the sciences and the mother of safety."*

Costs make the difference between investment success and investment failure. So, sharpen your pencils. Do your own arithmetic. Realize that you are not consigned to playing the hyperactive management game that is played by the overwhelming majority of individual investors and mutual fund owners alike. The low-cost index fund is there to guarantee that you will earn your fair share of whatever returns—positive or negative—our businesses earn and their stock prices and dividends deliver.

Don't Take My Word for It

The innate superiority of the index fund has been endorsed (perhaps grudgingly) by a wide range of mutual fund industry insiders. When he retired, here's what **Peter Lynch**, the legendary manager who steered Fidelity Magellan Fund to such great success during his 1977 to 1990 tenure, had to say in *Barron's*: "The S&P is up 343.8 percent for 10 years. That is a four-bagger. The general equity funds are up 283 percent. So it's getting worse, the deterioration by professionals is getting worse. *The public would be better off in an index fund.*"

* * *

Now hear industry leader **Jon Fossel**, former chairman of the Investment Company Institute and of the Oppenheimer Funds, in the *Wall Street Journal*: "People ought to recognize that the

(continued)

average fund can *never* outperform the market in total." (Italics added.)

* * *

Even hyperactive investors seem to believe in indexing strategies. Here's what **James J. Cramer**, money manager and host of CNBC's *Mad Money*, says: "After a lifetime of picking stocks, I have to admit that Bogle's arguments in favor of the index fund have me thinking of joining him rather than trying to beat him. Bogle's wisdom and common sense [are] indispensable . . . for anyone trying to figure out how to invest in this crazy stock market." (So far, Mr. Cramer doesn't seem to have taken his own advice.)

* * *

And even managers of alternative investments join the chorus. One of money management's giants, **Clifford S. Asness**, managing and founding principal of AQR Capital Management, adds his own wisdom, expertise, and integrity: "Market-cap based indexing will never be driven from its deserved perch as core and deserved king of the investment world. It is what we should all own in theory and it has delivered low-cost equity returns to a great mass of investors . . . *the now and forever king-of-the-hill.*"

Chapter Five

Focus on the Lowest-Cost Funds

~

The More the Managers Take, the Less the Investors Make.

NEARLY ALL FUND EXPERTS, advisers to investors, the financial media, and investors themselves rely heavily—indeed almost to the exclusion of other information—on selecting funds based on their past performance. But while past performance tells us what happened, it cannot tell us what *will* happen. Indeed, as you will later learn, emphasis on fund performance is not only *not* productive; it is counterproductive. Our own common sense, deep down, tells us: *Performance comes and goes.*

But there is one powerful factor in shaping fund returns, often ignored, that is essential to know: You can be more successful in selecting winning funds by focusing, not on the inevitable evanescence of past performance, but on something that seems to go on forever or, more fairly, a factor that has persisted in shaping fund returns throughout the fund industry's long history. That factor is the *cost* of owning mutual funds. *Costs go on forever.*

Fund performance comes and goes.
Costs go on forever.

What are these costs? The first and best known is the fund's expense ratio, and it tends to change little over time. Although some funds scale down their fee rates as assets grow, the reductions are usually sufficiently modest that high-cost funds (average expense ratio of the highest-cost decile funds, 2.40 percent) tend to remain high-cost; lower-cost funds tend to remain lower-cost (fourth decile average expense ratio, 0.98 percent), and the few very low-cost funds tend to remain very low-cost (lowest-cost decile average expense ratio, 0.32 percent). The average-cost funds in the fifth and sixth deciles (1.10 percent and 1.24 percent) also tend to persist in that category.

The second large cost of equity fund ownership is the sales charge paid on each purchase of shares. The drag of sales loads is almost invariably ignored in the published data, although it, too, tends to persist. Load funds rarely become no-load funds, and vice versa.[1] (I can recall no large fund organization making the immediate conversion from a load to a no-load distribution system since Vanguard took that unprecedented step way back in 1977.)

The third major cost incurred by fund investors is the cost of the purchase and sale of portfolio securities. These transactions cost money. We estimate that turnover costs are roughly 0.5 percent on each purchase and each sale, meaning that a fund with 100 percent portfolio turnover would carry a cost to shareholders of about 1 percent of assets, year after year. Similarly, 50 percent turnover would cost about 0.50 percent per year of a fund's returns. A 10 percent turnover would slash the cost to 0.10 percent, and so on.

---

[1] The use of front-end loads has diminished in recent years, often replaced by "spread loads" that sharply increase fund expense ratios. For example, the A share class offered by one of the largest mutual fund distributors carried a front-end load of 5.75 percent in 2016, and an expense ratio of 0.58 percent. The distributor now offers a new T-share class of its funds, carrying a front-end load of 2.5 percent plus an annual marketing cost of an additional 0.25 percent per year that must be paid for as long as the investor owns the shares. This annual fee will raise the fund's expense ratios to an estimated 0.83 percent.

Rule of thumb: assume that a fund's turnover costs equal 1 percent of the turnover rate. In 2016, purchases and sales of portfolio securities in equity mutual funds totaled $6.6 trillion, equal to 78 percent of average equity fund assets of $8.4 trillion. The cost of all that trading, often among competitors, came to something like $66 billion, an annual cost equal to 0.8 percent of fund assets.

---- ∽ ----

Costs are large, and too often ignored.

Most comparisons of fund costs focus solely on reported expense ratios, and uniformly find that higher costs are associated with lower returns. This pattern holds not only for equity funds as a group, but in each of the nine Morningstar style boxes (large-, mid-, and small-cap funds, each sorted into three fund groups with either growth, value, or blended objectives).

While few independent comparisons take into account the additional cost of fund portfolio turnover, a similar relationship exists. Funds in the lowest-turnover quartile have consistently outperformed those in the highest-turnover quartile for all equity funds as a group, and in each of the nine style boxes.

Adding these estimated turnover costs to each fund's expense ratio makes the relationship between fund costs and fund returns sheer dynamite. Taking into account both costs, we find that all-in annual costs of actively managed equity funds range from 0.9 percent of assets in the lowest-cost quartile to 2.3 percent in the highest-cost quartile, as shown in Exhibit 5.1. (This exercise ignores sales charges and therefore *overstates* the net returns earned by the funds in each quartile.)

Costs matter. A lot.

Costs matter! Exhibit 5.1 shows a 1.4 percent difference between the average expense ratio of funds in the highest-cost quartile and the lowest-cost funds. This cost differential largely explains the advantage in returns among the lowest-cost funds over the highest-cost funds. During the past 25 years: average net annual return of lowest-cost funds, 9.4 percent; net annual return of highest-cost funds, just 8.3 percent, an enhancement in return achieved simply by minimizing costs.

Note, too, that in each of the fund quartiles, when we add back fund costs to the funds' reported net returns, the gross annual returns earned in each category are virtually

EXHIBIT 5.1 Equity Mutual Funds: Returns versus Costs, 1991–2016

| | **Annual Rate** | | | | | | | **Risk-** |
| | | **Costs** | | | | | | **Adjusted** |
Cost Quartile	**Gross Return**	**Expense Ratio**	**Turnover (est.)**	**Total Costs**	**Net Return***	**Cumulative Return**	**Risk****	**Return**
One (lowest cost)	10.3%	0.71%	0.21%	0.91%	9.4%	855%	16.2%	8.9%
Two	10.6	0.99	0.31	1.30	9.3	818	17.0	8.4
Three	10.5	1.01	0.61	1.62	8.9	740	17.5	7.8
Four (highest cost)	10.6	1.44	0.90	2.34	8.3	632	17.4	7.4
500 Index Fund	9.2%	0.04%	0.04%	0.08%	9.1%	783%	15.3%	9.1%

*This analysis includes only funds that survived the full 25-year period. Thus, these data significantly overstate the results achieved by equity funds due to survivorship bias.

**Annual standard deviation of returns.

identical. Those gross returns (before costs) fall into a narrow range: 10.6 percent for the highest-cost quartile and 10.3 percent for the lowest-cost quartile, just what we might expect. *In each quartile costs account for essentially all of the differences in the annual net returns earned by the funds.*

There is yet another significant difference. As costs increase, so does risk. Using the volatility of annual returns as the measure of risk, the lowest-cost funds carried significantly less risk (average volatility of 16.2 percent) than their highest-cost peers (17.4 percent). When we take that reduction in risk into account, the risk-adjusted annual return for the lowest-cost quartile comes to 8.9 percent, fully 1.5 percentage points higher than the 7.4 percent risk-adjusted return of the highest-cost quartile.

The magic of compounding, again.

That 1.5 percent annual advantage in risk-adjusted return may not seem like much. But when we compound those annual returns over time, the cumulative difference reaches staggering proportions. The compound return for the period is 855 percent for the lowest-cost funds and 632 percent for the highest-cost funds, an increase of more than 35 percent, a superiority arising almost entirely from the cost differential. Talk about the relentless rules of humble arithmetic!

In other words, the final value of the lowest-cost funds multiplied the original investment more than eight-fold, while the highest-cost quartile returns were multiplied about sixfold. Surely "fishing in the low-cost pond" should enhance your returns, and by a wide margin at that. Again, yes, costs matter!

Are we overstating the importance of fund costs? I think not. These next few paragraphs from a respected analyst at Morningstar confirm my conclusions, and then some:

> If there's anything in the whole world of mutual funds that you can take to the bank, it's that expense ratios help you make a better decision. In every single time period and data point tested, low-cost funds beat high-cost funds.
>
> Expense ratios are strong predictors of performance. In every asset class over every time period, the cheapest quintile produced higher total returns than the most expensive quintile.
>
> Investors should make expense ratios a primary test in fund selection. They are still the most dependable predictor of performance. Start by focusing on funds in the cheapest or two cheapest quintiles, and you'll be on the path to success.

───────────────── ∽ ─────────────────

Low costs and index funds.

But if you are persuaded by this powerful affirmation that, yes, costs matter, and decide to focus on the lowest-cost group of funds, why limit the search to actively managed funds? Traditional index funds (TIFs) had the lowest costs of all: expenses averaging just 0.1 percent during this period. With no measurable turnover costs, its total all-in costs were but 0.1 percent. The gross return of the S&P 500 Index fund was 9.2 percent per year; the net return, 9.1 percent. Carrying a lower risk than any of the four cost quartiles (volatility 15.3 percent), its risk-adjusted annual return was also 9.1 percent, a cumulative gain that ranked the index fund ahead of even the lowest-cost quartile funds by 0.2 percent per year.

If the managers take nothing, the investors receive everything: the market's return.

Caution: The index fund's annual risk-adjusted return of 9.1 percent over the past 25 years is all the more impressive since the returns of the active equity funds are overstated (as always) by the fact that only the funds that were good enough to survive the decade are included in the data. Adjusted for this "survivorship bias," the return of the average equity fund would fall from 9.0 percent to an estimated 7.5 percent.

What's more, selecting the index fund eliminated the need to search for those rare needles in the market haystack represented by the very few active funds that have performed better than that haystack, in the often-vain hope that their winning ways will continue over decades yet to come.

As Morningstar suggests, if investors could rely on only a single factor to select future superior performers and to avoid future inferior performers, that factor would be fund costs. The record could hardly be clearer: *The more the managers and brokers take, the less the investors make.* Again, if the managers and brokers take *nothing*, the investors receive *everything* (i.e., the total return of the stock market).

Don't Take My Word for It

As far back as 1995, **Tyler Mathisen**, now Managing Editor of CNBC Business News, deserves credit for being among the first journalists—if not the first—to recognize the important role that mutual fund costs (expense ratios, turnover costs, and unnecessary taxes) play in eroding the returns delivered to mutual fund shareholders. Mathisen, then executive editor of *Money*, conceded the superiority of the low-cost, low-turnover, tax-efficient index fund:

"For nearly two decades, John Bogle, the tart-tongued chairman of the Vanguard Group, has preached the virtues of index funds—those boring portfolios that aim to match the performance of a market barometer. And for much of that time, millions of fund investors (not to mention dozens of financial journalists including this one) basically ignored him.

"Sure, we recognized the intrinsic merits of index funds such as low annual expenses and because the funds keep turnover to a minimum, tiny transaction costs. Moreover, because index fund managers convert paper profits into realized gains less frequently than do the skippers of actively managed funds, shareholders pay less tax each year to Uncle Sam. To be sure, those three advantages form a trio as impressive as Domingo, Pavarotti, and Carreras.

"Well, Jack, we were wrong. You win. Settling for average is good enough, at least for a substantial portion of most investors' stock and bond portfolios. In fact, more often than not, aiming for benchmark-matching returns through index funds

(continued)

assures shareholders of a better-than-average chance of outperforming the typical managed stock or bond portfolio. It's the paradox of fund investing today: Gunning for average is your best shot at finishing above average.

"We've come around to agreeing with the sometimes prickly, always provocative, fund exec known to admirers and detractors alike as Saint Jack: Indexing should form the core of most investors' fund portfolios. So here's to you, Jack. You have a right to call it, as you recently did in a booklet you wrote, *The Triumph of Indexing*."

(Thanks, Tyler!)

Chapter Six

Dividends Are the Investor's (Best?) Friend

--- ∽ ---

*But Mutual Funds Confiscate
Too Much of Them.*

DIVIDEND YIELDS ARE A vital part of the long-term return generated by the stock market. In fact, since 1926 (the first year for which we have comprehensive data on the S&P 500 Index), dividends have contributed an average annual return of 4.2 percent, accounting for fully 42 percent of the stock market's annual return of 10.0 percent for the period.

An astonishing revelation.

Compounded over that long span, dividends made a contribution to the market's appreciation that is almost beyond belief. Excluding dividend income, an initial investment of $10,000 in the S&P 500 on January 1, 1926, would have grown to more than $1.7 million as 2017 began. But with dividends reinvested, that investment would have grown to some $59.1 million! This astonishing gap of $57.4 million between (1) market price appreciation alone and (2) total return when dividends are reinvested simply reflects (once again) "the magic of cost-free compounding" (Exhibit 6.1).

The stability of the annual dividends per share of the S&P 500 is truly remarkable (Exhibit 6.2). Over the 90-year span beginning in 1926, there were only three significant drops: (1) a 55 percent decline during the first years of the Great Depression (1929–1933); (2) a 36 percent decline in the Depression's aftermath in 1938; and (3) a 21 percent decline during the global financial crisis of 2008–2009. This most recent decline occurred largely because banks were forced to eliminate their dividends. Dividends per share on the 500 Index fell from $28.39 in 2008 to $22.41 in 2009, but reached a new high of $45.70 in 2016, 60 percent above the earlier peak in 2008.

EXHIBIT 6.1   S&P Price Return versus Total Return

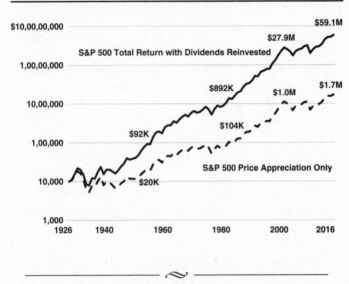

Mutual fund managers give dividend income
a low priority.

Given the obvious power of compounding dividends over the long term and the relative stability of corporate dividend payouts, actively managed mutual funds must give dividend income a high priority. Right?

Wrong! Because mutual fund management contracts consistently call for advisory fees that are based on a fund's *net assets*—not on its *dividend income*. When stock market dividend yields are low (as in recent years), fund expenses

EXHIBIT 6.2   S&P 500—Dividends per Share

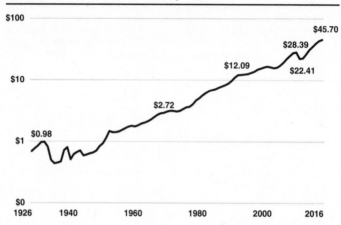

consume a huge share of the total dividend income earned by funds.

The result: a staggering proportion of equity fund dividend income is consumed by expenses. "Staggering" is no overstatement. In actively managed growth funds, expenses actually consume 100 percent(!) of fund income. In actively managed value funds, expenses consume 58 percent of dividend income.

The contrast between actively managed funds and comparable index funds is stark. The comparable value index fund expenses consumed 2 percent of fund income in 2016; the expenses on a low-cost growth index fund consumed just 4 percent (Exhibit 6.3).

EXHIBIT 6.3   Dividend Yields and Fund Expenses, 2016

Actively Managed Funds	Gross Yield	Expense Ratio	Net Yield	Share of Gross Yield Consumed by Expenses
Growth funds	1.3%	1.3%	0.0%	100%
Value funds	2.1	1.2	0.9	58
Low-Cost Index Funds				
Growth funds	1.4%	0.1%	1.3%	4%
Value funds	2.5	0.1	2.4	2

Source: Morningstar.

———————————— ∾ ————————————

Actively managed equity funds confiscate your dividend income.

Despite the powerful impact of dividends on long-term returns, you, like nearly all investors, are likely unaware of this astonishing confiscation of dividend income. How *could* you know? While it may be possible to calculate these data from a fund's financial statements, those statements are hardly beacons of full, clear, and forthright disclosure.

So why not consider a low-cost index fund, which has no active portfolio manager; has an annual expense ratio as low as 0.04 percent; which delivers your fair share of the fund's dividend income; and does virtually no trading of stocks through those Helpers mentioned at the outset? Why not, indeed? Chapter 13 explores this idea further.

Don't Take My Word for It

A blogger who goes by the name "**Dividend Growth Investor**" picked up on my message about the importance of dividends and wrote an article that echoes my dividend philosophy.

"John Bogle is an investing legend. . . . I have read several of his books, and really enjoyed his simple messages. I really liked Bogle's message on keeping costs low, keeping turnover low, staying the course, and keeping it simple. I liked the advice the minute I read it. . . . I especially liked Bogle's advice on dividends.

"Bogle is an advocate of focusing on the dividend payments, and ignoring stock price fluctuations. He points out that the stock market is a giant distraction, and that investors should keep an eye on the dividends. . . .

"He correctly points out that dividends have a smooth uptrend over time. This makes dividends an ideal source of dependable income for retirees. . . . Bogle also mentions that while dividends are not guaranteed, they have gone down more noticeably only a couple of times in the past....

"I really love his overall message on staying the course, focusing on dividends, keeping investment costs low, and ignoring stock prices. He also believes in keeping things simple. Bogle is against the widespread practice today of building portfolios that consist of 10–15 asset classes, whose sole purpose is to create complexity to generate fees for greedy asset managers. Keeping it simple means owning stocks and some bonds. It also means not getting too fancy and too carried away by adding fashionable asset classes whose merits are derived from a backtested computer model."

Chapter Seven

The Grand Illusion

~

*Surprise! The Returns Reported by
Mutual Funds Are Rarely Earned by
Mutual Fund Investors.*

IT IS GRATIFYING THAT industry insiders such as Fidelity's Peter Lynch, former Investment Company Institute (ICI) chairman Jon Fossel, *Mad Money's* James Cramer, and AQR's Clifford Asness agree with me, as you may recall from Chapter 4. The returns earned by the typical equity mutual fund are inevitably inadequate relative to the returns available simply by owning the stock market through an index fund based on the S&P 500.

But the idea that fund investors *themselves* actually earn 100 percent of those inadequate mutual fund returns proves to be a grand illusion. Not only an illusion, but a generous one. The reality is considerably worse. For in addition to paying the heavy costs that fund managers extract for their services, the shareholders pay an additional cost that has been even larger. In this chapter, we'll explain why.

Fund managers typically report the traditional *time-weighted* returns calculated by their funds—the change in the asset value of each fund share, adjusted to reflect the reinvestment of all income dividends and any capital gains distributions. Over the past 25 years, the average mutual fund earned a return of 7.8 percent per year—1.3 percentage points less than the 9.1 percent return of the S&P 500. But that *fund* return does not tell us what return was earned by the average fund *investor*. And that return turns out to be far lower.

Hint: Money flows into most funds *after* good performance, and goes out when bad performance follows.

To ascertain the return earned by the average fund investor, we must consider the *dollar-weighted* return, which accounts for the impact of capital flows from investors, into and out of the fund.[1] (Hint: Money flows into most funds after good performance is achieved, and goes out when bad performance follows.)

When we compare traditionally calculated fund returns with the returns actually earned by their investors over the past quarter century, it turns out that the average fund investor earned, not the 7.8 percent return reported by the average fund, but 6.3 percent—an annual return fully 1.5 percentage points per year less than that of the fund.

The index fund investor, too, was enticed by the rising market, but still earned a return of 8.8 percent, only 0.2 percentage points short of the fund return itself.

Yes, during the past 25 years, while the S&P 500 Index was providing an annual return of 9.1 percent and the average equity *fund* was earning an annual return of 7.8 percent, the average fund *investor* was earning only 6.3 percent a year.

———————————— ∿ ————————————

The dual penalties of costs and investor behavior.

———————————————————————————

[1] Extreme example: If a fund with $100 million of assets earns a time-weighted return of 30 percent on its net asset value during a given year, and investors, recognizing the strong return, purchase $1 billion worth of its shares on the final day of the year, the average dollar-weighted return earned by its investors would be just 4.9 percent.

Compounded over the full period, the 1.5 percent annual penalty incurred by the average fund because of costs was huge. But the dual penalties of faulty timing and adverse selection made it even larger.

Exhibit 7.1 shows that $10,000 invested in a low-cost S&P 500 index fund in 1991 earned a nominal (before-inflation) profit of $77,000. The average equity fund earned a profit of just $55,500—72 percent of what was there for the taking. The compound return earned by the average fund investor tumbled to $36,100, less than 50 percent of the $73,100 return earned by investors in the simple index fund. These penalties add up!

EXHIBIT 7.1   S&P Index Fund versus Average Large-Cap Fund: Profit on Initial Investment of $10,000, 1991–2016

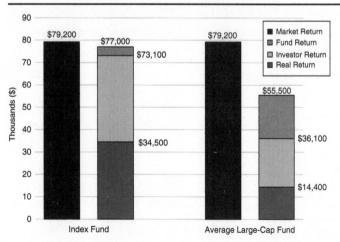

When we take inflation into account, the value of all those dollars tumbles. With inflation that averaged 2.7 percent annually, the index fund *real* return drops to 6.2 percent per year, but the real return of the average fund investor plummets to just 3.6 percent—a cumulative $34,500 of real value for the index fund versus just $14,400 for the fund investor. Truth be told, it's hard to imagine such a staggering gap. But the facts are the facts.

While the data clearly indicate that fund investor returns fell well short of fund returns, there is no way to be precise about the exact shortfall.[2] But the point of this examination of the returns earned by the stock market, the average fund, and the average fund owner is designed not for *precision*, but for *direction*.

Whatever the precise data, the evidence is compelling that (1) the long-term returns on equity funds lag the stock market by a substantial amount, largely accounted for by their costs; and (2) the returns earned by fund investors lag the market by *more than double* that substantial lag.

---

[2] This gap was estimated based on the difference between the time-weighted returns reported by Morningstar on the average large-cap fund and actual dollar-weighted returns over the full 25-year period.

---------------------------- ∼ ----------------------------

Inflamed by heady optimism and greed, and enticed by the wiles of mutual fund marketers, investors poured their savings into equity funds at the bull market peak.

What explains this second shocking lag? Simply put, counterproductive market timing and adverse fund selection. First, shareholders investing in equity funds paid a heavy timing penalty. They invested too little of their savings in equity funds when stocks represented good values during the 1980s and early 1990s. Then, inflamed by the heady optimism and greed of the era and enticed by the wiles of mutual fund marketers as the bull market neared its peak, they poured too much of their savings into equity funds.

Second, they paid a selection penalty, pouring their money not only into the market at the wrong time, but into the wrong funds—funds that had provided outstanding results in the past, but, as we shall soon see, tumbled thereafter. Why? Simply because high fund returns tend to revert toward or below the mean of average returns. (We'll discuss reversion to the mean—RTM—in Chapter 11.) With both counterproductive timing and poor fund selection, investors simply fail to practice what common sense would have told them.

—————————— ≈ ——————————

When counterproductive investor emotions are magnified by counterproductive fund industry promotions, little good is apt to result.

——————————————————————————

This lag effect has been amazingly pervasive. For example, the returns provided to investors from 2008 to 2016 by 186 of the 200 largest equity funds were lower than the returns that they reported to investors!

This lag was especially evident during the "new economy" craze of the late 1990s. Then, the fund industry organized more and more funds, usually funds that carried considerably higher risk than the stock market itself, and magnified the problem by heavily advertising the eye-catching past returns earned by the hottest funds.

As the market soared, investors poured ever larger sums of money into equity funds. They invested a net total of only $18 billion in 1990 when stocks were cheap, but $420 billion in 1999 and 2000, when stocks were substantially overvalued (Exhibit 7.2).

What's more, investors also overwhelmingly chose "new economy" funds, technology funds, and the hottest-performing growth funds, to the virtual exclusion of more conservative value-oriented funds. Whereas only 20 percent of their money had been invested in risky aggressive

EXHIBIT 7.2   The Timing and Selection Penalties: Net Flow into U.S. Equity Funds

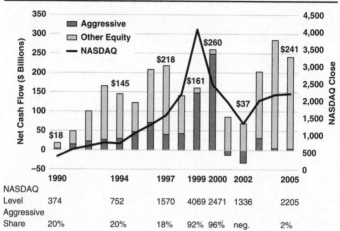

NASDAQ	1990	1994	1997	1999	2000	2002	2005
Level	374	752	1570	4069	2471	1336	2205
Aggressive Share	20%	20%	18%	92%	96%	neg.	2%

growth funds in 1990, investors poured fully 95 percent into such funds as those fund returns peaked during 1999 and early 2000. After the bubble burst, when it was too late, investor purchases dried up to as little as $36 billion in 2002, just before the market hit bottom. They also pulled their money out of growth funds and turned, too late, to value funds.

The underwhelming performance of fund investors returned during the financial crisis of 2008–2009 and the subsequent recovery. Fund investors have been chasing past performance since time immemorial, allowing their emotions—perhaps even their greed—to overwhelm their reason. Many investors reacted strongly—and ultimately counterproductively—to the sharp downturn in the markets during the financial crisis by getting out of stocks near the market's nadir. Many of those investors missed part or even all of the subsequent recovery, a cumulative increase by the end of 2016 of some 250 percent from the low.

Investor emotions plus fund industry promotions equals trouble.

The fund industry itself has compounded the problem by playing on investors' emotions, bringing out new funds to meet the fads and fashions of the day (often supercharged and speculative), and then aggressively advertising and marketing them. It is fair to say that when counterproductive investor emotions are played upon by counterproductive fund industry promotions, little good is apt to result.

The fund industry will not soon give up on its new products or its promotions, and it will take time (and first-hand experience) by investors with counterproductive short-term behavior to gain wisdom. But the intelligent investor will be well advised to heed not only the message in Chapter 4 about minimizing expenses, but the message in this chapter about removing emotions from the equation—that is, about investors improving their short-term, market-oriented behavior.

The beauty of the index fund, then, lies not only in its low expenses, but in its elimination of all those tempting fund choices that promise so much and deliver so little. Focusing on the long term, doing one's best to ignore the short-term noise of the stock market, and eschewing the hot funds of the day, the index fund can be held through thick and thin for an investment lifetime. Emotions need never enter the equation. The winning formula for success in investing is owning the entire stock market through an index fund, and then doing nothing. Just stay the course.

Don't Take My Word for It

The wise **Warren Buffett** shares my view. Consider what I call his *four E's.* "The greatest Enemies of the Equity investor are Expenses and Emotions." So does **Andrew Lo,** MIT professor and author of *Adaptive Markets* (2017), who personally "invests by buying and holding index funds."

* * *

Perhaps even more surprisingly, the founder and chief executive of the largest mutual fund supermarket—while vigorously promoting stock trading and actively managed funds—favors the classic index fund for himself. When asked why people invest in managed funds, **Charles Schwab** answered: "It's fun to play around . . . it's human nature to try to select the right horse . . . [But] for the average person, I'm more of an indexer. . . . The predictability is so high. . . . For 10, 15, 20 years you'll be in the 85th percentile of performance. Why would you screw it up?" (Most of Mr. Schwab's personal portfolio is invested in index funds.)

* * *

Mark Hulbert, editor of the highly regarded *Hulbert Financial Digest*, concurs. "Assuming that the future is like the past, you can outperform 80 percent of your fellow investors over the next several decades by investing in an index fund—and doing nothing else. . . . [A]cquire the discipline to do something even better [than trying to beat the market]: become a long-term index fund investor." His *New York Times* article was headlined: "Buy and Hold? Sure, but Don't Forget the 'Hold.'"

Chapter Eight

Taxes Are Costs, Too

~

*Don't Pay Uncle Sam Any More Than
You Should.*

WE STILL AREN'T THROUGH with these relentless rules of
humble arithmetic, the logical, inevitable, and unyielding
long-term penalties assessed against stock market participants by investment expenses, the powerful impact of
inflation, counterproductive investor behavior, and fund
industry promotion of untested and "hot" mutual funds.
These practices have slashed the capital accumulated by
mutual fund investors. The index fund has provided excellent protection from the penalty of nearly all of these hidden costs. (Of course, the index fund's real returns were

not exempt from the ravages of inflation, which impact all investments equally.)

But there is yet another cost—too often ignored—that slashes even further the net returns that investors actually receive. I'm referring to taxes—federal, state, and local income taxes.[1] And here again, the index fund garners a substantial edge. The fact is that most managed mutual funds are astonishingly tax-inefficient Why? Because of the short-term focus of their portfolio managers, who too often are frenetic traders of the stocks in the portfolios that they supervise.

~

Managed mutual funds are astonishingly tax-inefficient.

The portfolio turnover of the average actively managed equity fund, including both purchases and sales, now comes to 78 percent per year. (The "traditional" turnover rate—which includes only the lesser of purchases or sales—is 39 percent.) Industrywide, the average stock

---

[1] About one-half of all equity mutual fund shares are held by individual investors in fully taxable investment accounts. The other half are held in tax-deferred accounts such as individual retirement accounts (IRAs) and corporate savings, thrift, and profit-sharing plans. If your fund holdings are solely in the latter category, you need not be concerned with the discussion in this chapter.

is held by the average active fund for an average of just 19 months. (Based on total assets, the average holding period is 31 months.) Hard as it is to imagine, from 1945 to 1965 the annual turnover rate of equity funds averaged just 16 percent, an average holding period of six years for the average stock in a fund portfolio. This huge increase in turnover and its attendant transaction costs have ill-served fund investors. But the baneful impact of excessive taxes that funds have passed through to their investors have made a bad situation worse.

This pattern of tax inefficiency for active managers seems destined to continue as long as (1) stocks rise and (2) fund managers continue their pattern of hyperactive trading. Let's be clear: In an earlier era, most fund managers focused on long-term investment. Now they are too often focused on short-term speculation. The traditional index fund follows precisely the opposite policy—buying and holding "forever." Its annual portfolio turnover has run in the range of 3 percent, resulting in transaction costs that are somewhere between infinitesimal and zero.

―――――――――― ∼ ――――――――――

Bring on the data!

So let's pick up where we left off a few chapters ago. Recall that the net annual return was 7.8 percent for the average equity fund over the past 25 years and 9.0 percent for the S&P 500 index fund. With the high portfolio turnover of actively managed funds, their taxable investors were subject to an estimated effective annual federal tax of 1.2 percentage points per year, or about 15 percent of their total pre-tax return. (State and local taxes would further balloon the figure.) Result: their after-tax annual return was cut to 6.6 percent.

Despite the higher returns that they earned, investors in the index fund were actually subjected to lower taxes, largely derived from their dividend income. The extremely low costs of index funds consume less dividend income relative to actively managed funds, resulting in higher dividend yields and, therefore, higher taxes on dividends.

In mid-2017, the dividend yield on a low-cost Standard & Poor's 500 index fund totaled 2.0 percent, *double* the yield on the average actively managed equity fund. Federal taxes cost taxable investors in index funds about 0.45 percent per year, only about one-third of the 1.5 percent annual tax burden borne by investors in actively managed funds.

Given that active funds often distribute substantial short-term capital gains to their shareholders—which are taxed at higher ordinary income rates, not the lower long-term capital gains rate—investors in active funds face substantial tax burdens that index investors do not face.

Result: The average actively managed equity fund earned an annual after-tax return of 6.6 percent, compared to 8.6 percent for the index investor. Compounded, an initial 1991 investment of $10,000 generated a profit of $39,700 after taxes for the active funds, less than 60 percent of the $68,300 of accumulated growth in the index fund. The active fund lag: a loss to their investors of some $28,600.[2]

∼

Fund returns are devastated by costs, adverse fund selections, bad timing, taxes, and inflation.

I hesitate to assign to any single one of these negative factors the responsibility for being "the straw that broke the camel's back" of equity fund returns. But surely the final straws include (1) high costs (Chapters 4, 5, and 6), (2) adverse investor selections and counterproductive market timing (Chapter 7), and (3) taxes (Chapter 8). Whichever way one looks at it, the camel's back is surely broken. But the very last straw, it turns out, is inflation.

---

[2] The index fund investor would be subject to taxes on any gains realized when liquidating shares. But for an investor who bequeaths shares to heirs, the cost would be "stepped up" to their market value on date of death, and no capital gain would be recognized or taxed.

~

Nominal returns versus real returns.

When we pay our fund costs in *current* dollars, year after year—and that's exactly how we pay our fund expenses and our taxes on fund capital gains (often realized on a short-term basis, to boot)—and yet accumulate our assets only in *real* dollars, eroded by the relentless rise in the cost of living that has been embedded in our economy, the results are devastating.

It is truly remarkable—and hardly praiseworthy—that this devastation is so often ignored in the information that mutual funds provide to their investors.

A paradox: While the index fund is remarkably tax-*efficient* in managing capital gains, it turns out to be relatively tax-*inefficient* in distributing dividend income. Why? Because its rock-bottom costs mean that nearly all of the dividends paid on the stocks held by the low-cost index fund flow directly into the hands of the index fund's shareholders.

Don't Take My Word for It

Consider these words from a paper by **John B. Shoven**, of Stanford University and the National

Bureau of Economic Research, and **Joel M. Dickson**, then of the Federal Reserve System (now a principal at Vanguard): "Mutual funds have failed to manage their realized capital gains in such a way as to permit a substantial deferral of taxes, [raising] investors' tax bills considerably. . . . If the Vanguard 500 Index Fund could have deferred all of its realized capital gains, it would have ended up in the 91.8th percentile for the high-tax investor" (i.e., outpaced 92 percent of all managed equity funds).

* * *

Or listen to investment adviser **William Bernstein**, author of *The Four Pillars of Investing*: "While it is probably a poor idea to own actively managed mutual funds in general, it is truly a *terrible* idea to own them in taxable accounts . . . [taxes are] a drag on performance of up to 4 percentage points each year . . . many index funds allow your capital gains to grow largely undisturbed until you sell. . . . *For the taxable investor, indexing means never having to say you're sorry.*"

* * *

(continued)

And **Burton G. Malkiel** again casts his lot with the index fund: "Index funds are ... tax friendly, allowing investors to defer the realization of capital gains or avoid them completely if the shares are later bequeathed. To the extent that the long-run uptrend in stock prices continues, switching from security to security involves realizing capital gains that are subject to tax. Taxes are a crucially important financial consideration because the earlier realization of capital gains will substantially reduce net returns. Index funds do not trade from security to security and, thus, they tend to avoid capital gains taxes."

Chapter Nine

When the Good Times No Longer Roll

~

It's Wise to Plan on Lower Future Returns in the Stock and Bond Markets.

REMEMBER THE UNFAILING PRINCIPLE described in Chapter 2: In the long run it is the reality of business—the dividend yields and earnings growth of corporations—that drives the returns generated by the stock market. Paradoxically, however, if we simply consider only the 43 years since I founded Vanguard on September 24, 1974, the returns provided by the stock market exceeded the returns earned by businesses by among the highest margins in any period of such length in the entire history of the U.S. market.

Specifically, the dividend yields and earnings growth of the public corporations that compose the Standard & Poor's 500 Index created an *investment* return of but 8.8 percent during that period (dividend yield 3.3 percent, earnings growth 5.5 percent), yet the total annual return was 11.7 percent. (See Exhibit 9.1.)

Fully 2.9 percentage points of the market's return—fully 25 percent of the total—were accounted for by speculative return. That return reflected an upward revaluation of stocks by investors, as the price/earnings multiple more than tripled, from 7.5 times earnings to 23.7 times. (The average decade-long contribution of speculative return to the market's total annual return since 1900 has been but 0.5 percentage points, only about one-fifth of the bounty that we investors have enjoyed since 1974.)

The cumulative effects of these compounding returns are staggering (Exhibit 9.1). Over that 43-year period, an initial investment of $10,000 would have grown to just under $1,090,000. Of that million-dollar-plus accumulation, about $270,000 can be attributed to speculative return, while the remaining $820,000 was due to dividends and earnings growth.

Yes, that remarkably low P/E multiple of 7.5 times in September 1974 came at the bottom of a 50 percent

EXHIBIT 9.1   Cumulative Investment Return and Speculative Return, 1900–2016

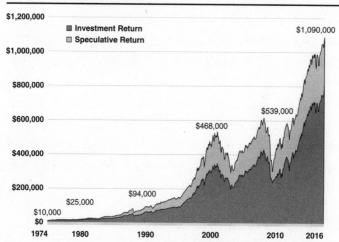

The staggering cumulative effects of compounding returns.

tumble in the stock market. It reflected deep pessimism, excessive fear, and widespread worry among investors. As 2017 begins, it remains to be seen whether the current valuation of 23.7 times earnings represents some combination of unbridled optimism, excessive confidence, exuberance, and hope, or a new reality.

———————— ∽ ————————

Both common sense and humble arithmetic tell us that we're facing an era of subdued returns in the stock market.

On balance over more than four decades, equity investors have enjoyed extraordinary returns. But since speculative return was responsible for fully 25 percent of the market's annual return during this period, it is unrealistic to expect P/E multiple expansion to repeat that performance, nor to give much, if any, momentum to the investment returns earned by stocks in the decade ahead. Common sense tells us that compared to the long-term annual nominal return of 9.5 percent since 1900, we're again facing an era of subdued returns in the stock market (Exhibit 9.2).

EXHIBIT 9.2   Total Return on Stocks, Past and Future

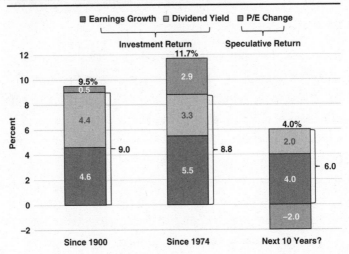

I say *again* because in the first (2007) edition of this book, I used the same title for this chapter, "When the Good Times No Longer Roll." There, I set reasonable expectations for the return on stocks over the 2006–2016 decade at 7 percent per year. The actual return on the S&P 500 was almost identical: 6.9 percent. (Hold the applause. I underestimated speculative return by about the same amount as I overestimated investment return.)

The arithmetic behind the caution: the sources of stock returns.

Why the continued caution? Simply because the sources of stock returns tell us to be cautious. Recall Lord Keynes's warning cited in Chapter 2, that "It is dangerous . . . to apply to the future inductive arguments based on past experience, unless one can distinguish the broad reasons for why past experience was what it was." In that chapter, I described three sources of return on stocks: the initial dividend yield and the earnings growth (together, "investment return"), and changes in the P/E multiple ("speculative return").

∾

Future annual investment return—6 percent?

Let's consider the sources of return as they appear today. First, today's dividend yield on stocks is not 4.4 percent (the historical rate), but 2 percent. Thus we can expect a deadweight loss of 2.4 percentage points per year in the contribution of dividend income to investment return.

As for corporate earnings, let's assume that they will continue to grow (as, over time, they usually have) at about the pace of our economy's expected *nominal* growth rate of 4 percent to 5 percent per year in gross domestic product (GDP) over the coming decade, below our nation's long-term nominal growth rate of 6 percent plus.

If that expectation proves to be reasonably accurate, then the most likely expectation for the investment return on stocks would be in the range of 6 percent to 7 percent. I'll be cautious and project an annual *investment* return averaging 6 percent.

∾

Future annual speculative return—*minus* 2 percent?

Now consider *speculative* return. As 2017 began, the price/earnings multiple on stocks was 23.7 times. That figure is based on the *past year's reported earnings* of the S&P 500. If the P/E ratio remains at that level a decade hence, *speculative* return would neither add to nor subtract from that possible 6 percent investment return.

Wall Street strategists generally prefer to calculate the P/E using *projected operating earnings for the coming year*, rather than *past reported earnings*. Such operating earnings exclude write-offs for discontinued business activities and other bad stuff, and projections of future earnings that may or may not be realized. Using projected operating earnings, Wall Street's P/E ratio is only 17 times. I would disregard that projection.

My guess—an informed guess, but still a guess—is that, by decade's end, the P/E ratio might ease down to, say, 20 times or even less. Such a revaluation would reduce the market's return by about 2 percentage points per year, resulting in an annual rate of return of 4 percent for the U.S. stock market.

If you don't agree with my 4 percent expectation, "do it yourself."

You don't have to agree with me. If you think today's P/E multiple of 23.7 will be unchanged a decade hence, speculative return would be zero, and the investment return would represent the market's entire return. If you expect the valuation to rise to 30 times (I don't), *add* 1.5 percentage points, bringing the annual return on stocks to 7.5 percent. If you think the P/E will drop to 12 times, *subtract* 7 percentage points, reducing the total nominal return on stocks to *minus* 1 percent.

My point is that you don't need to accept my cautious scenario. Feel free to disagree. Project the coming decade for yourself by applying the current dividend yield (there's no escaping that!), your own rational expectations for earnings growth, and your own view of the P/E ratio in 2027. That total will represent your own reasonable expectation for stock returns over the coming decade.

The source of bond returns—the current interest yield.

Developing reasonable expectations for future returns on bonds is even simpler than for stocks. Why? Because while stock returns have the three sources identified earlier, bond returns have a single dominant source: the interest rate prevailing when the bonds are purchased.

EXHIBIT 9.3   Initial Bond Yields and Subsequent Returns

Yes, the current yield on a bond (or a portfolio of bonds) represents the expected return if the bond is held for the long term. Historically, the initial yield has proved to be a reliable indicator of future returns. In fact, fully 95 percent of the decade-long returns on bonds since 1900 have been explained by the initial yield (Exhibit 9.3). Of course!

Why is this so? Because the issuer of a 10-year bond is pledged to repay its initial principal at 100 cents on the dollar at the end of a decade, and for investment-grade bonds, that promise has usually been fulfilled. So virtually all of its return is derived from interest payments. Yes, in

EXHIBIT 9.4   Total Return on Bonds, Past and Future

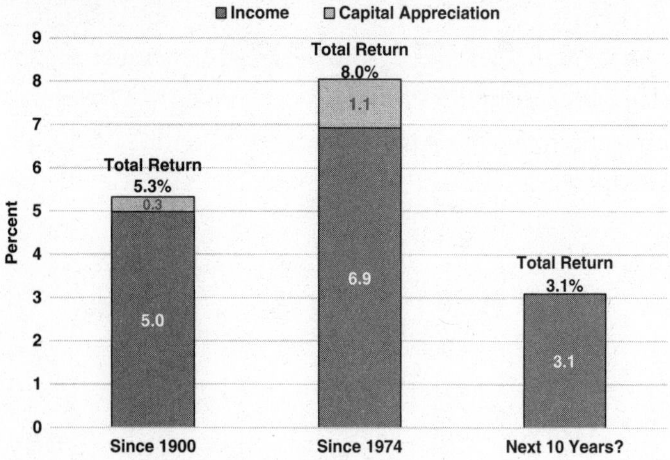

the interim the market value of the bond will vary with changing levels of interest rates. But when the bond is held to maturity, those fluctuations don't matter.

Exhibit 9.3 depicts the remarkably close relationship between the initial yield on the 10-year U.S. Treasury note and its subsequent 10-year return. Note the long cycle of its yields (and subsequent returns) from a low of 0.6 percent in 1940 to a high of 14.0 percent (amazing!) in 1981, then falling all the way back to 1.8 percent in 2012, before rebounding slightly to 2.2 percent in mid-2017.

The Treasury note carries minimal (or less!) risk of repayment, that is, the risk that the principal value of the bond will not be repaid when the bond matures. So its current yield of 2.2 percent significantly understates the future returns on the broad bond market, because corporate bonds assume higher repayment risk. So I'll develop my expectation for future returns on bonds based on a portfolio consisting of 50 percent U.S. Treasury notes now yielding 2.2 percent and 50 percent long-term investment-grade corporate bonds now yielding 3.9 percent. This combination produces a 3.1 percent yield on a broadly diversified bond portfolio. So, reasonable expectations suggest an annual return of 3.1 percent on bonds over the next decade.

During the coming decade, the returns on bonds, like the returns on stocks, are likely to fall well short of historical norms (Exhibit 9.4). Over the long sweep of history since 1900, the annual return on bonds has averaged 5.3 percent. During the modern era since 1974, the return on bonds has been far higher, averaging 8.0 percent annually. That return has been driven largely by the long, steady bull market that began in 1982 as interest rates tumbled and prices rose.

───────────────── ∽ ─────────────────

With lower returns are in prospect for stocks and bonds, balanced stock/bond portfolios will follow suit.

EXHIBIT 9.5   Total Return on 60/40 Stock/Bond Balanced Portfolio, Past and Future

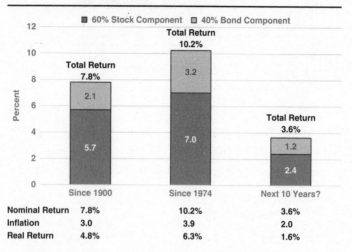

	Since 1900	Since 1974	Next 10 Years?
Nominal Return	7.8%	10.2%	3.6%
Inflation	3.0	3.9	2.0
Real Return	4.8%	6.3%	1.6%

Combining those reasonable expectations for future returns on stocks and bonds into a balanced portfolio consisting of 60 percent stocks and 40 percent bonds would give the expectation of a gross nominal annual return of 3.6 percent over the coming decade, before the deduction of investment costs. Of course, that expectation may prove to be too low or too high. But it may help to provide a realistic basis for your financial planning.

In any case, that 3.6 percent expected annual return would fall well below the long-term average for such a balanced portfolio of 7.8 percent and the remarkable 10.2 percent return since 1974 (Exhibit 9.5).

When we convert these nominal annual returns into real (after-inflation) returns, we see a smaller, yet still substantial gap: historical, 4.8 percent; since 1974, 6.3 percent; coming decade, maybe 1.6 percent. (See the table at the base of Exhibit 9.5.)

~

If rational expectations suggest a future gross annual return of 3.6 percent for a balanced fund, what does this imply for the net return to owners of the balanced fund?

In mid-2017, let's assume that 3.6 percent return is a rational expectation (*not* a prediction!) for annual returns on a balanced portfolio during the coming decade. But remember, please, that investors as a group can't (and don't) capture market returns in their entirety. Why? Simply because investing in the stock and bond markets through actively managed funds carries an estimated annual cost of at least 1.5 percent.

To calculate the likely return for the average actively managed balanced mutual fund in such an environment, simply remember the humble arithmetic of fund investing: nominal market return, minus investment costs, minus an assumed inflation rate of 2 percent (slightly above the rate that the financial markets are now expecting over the coming decade) equals just 0.1 percent per year. Here's the arithmetic:

Nominal gross return	3.6%
Investment costs	−1.5
Nominal net return	2.1%
Inflation	−2.0
Real annual return	0.1%

It may seem absurd to project a return of almost zero for the typical balanced fund. But, if you will recall the lesson learned in Chapter 7, the average balanced fund *investor* will earn even less. The numbers are there.

By way of comparison, in an environment of lower returns, a low-cost balanced index fund with annual costs of only 0.1 percent could provide a real annual return of, say, 1.5 percent—significantly higher than an actively managed fund. Not great, but at least positive, and almost infinitely better.

───────────── ∿ ─────────────

Unless the fund industry begins to change, the typical actively managed fund appears to be a singularly unfortunate investment choice.

───────────────────────────────

The fact is that lower returns harshly magnify the relentless arithmetic of excessive mutual fund costs. Why? Equity mutual fund costs of 2 percent combined with inflation of 2 percent would consume "only" about 25 percent of a 15 percent nominal return on stocks and "only" 40 percent of a 10 percent return. But costs and inflation would consume (I hope you're sitting down!) 100 percent of the 4 percent nominal return on stocks that rational expectations suggest.

Unless the fund industry begins to change—by sharply reducing management fees, operating expenses, sales charges, and portfolio turnover (and its attendant costs)—high-cost actively managed funds appear to be a singularly unfortunate choice for investors.

A zero real return achieved by the average active equity fund should be unacceptable. What can equity fund investors do to avoid being trapped by these relentless rules of humble arithmetic? How can they avoid the financial devastation that follows when high investment costs are applied to future returns that are likely to be well below long-term norms?

Five ways to avoid financial devastation. Only two work.

Here are five tempting options for improving your investment returns:

1. Select a very low-cost index fund that simply holds the stock market portfolio.
2. Select funds with rock-bottom costs, minimal portfolio turnover, and no sales loads.
3. Select winning funds on the basis of their past long-term records.
4. Select winning funds on the basis of their recent short-term performance.
5. Get some professional advice in selecting funds that are likely to outpace the market.

Which option will you choose? Hint: The odds are high that the first two options will virtually assure your investment success in capturing whatever returns that our financial markets prove to provide. The odds of success for the final three options are pitiful. We'll discuss the limitations of each in the following three chapters.

Don't Take My Word for It

Nearly every economist, academic, and stock market strategist who seriously studies the financial markets joins me in concluding that, yes, the good times we've enjoyed in the stock market since the lows were reached in the autumn of 1974 will "no longer roll" during the longer-term future.

Consider these projections from **AQR Capital Management**, one of the largest and most successful managers of alternative investments: "Expected investment returns are low. We expect a real return of 4.0 percent on equities and 0.5 percent on bonds, a 2.6 percent real return [before investment costs] on a 60/40 stock/bond portfolio."

* * *

These projections by AQR doubtless seem ragingly bullish next to those of **Jeremy Grantham**, longtime leader of GMO, an adviser to major endowment funds. Over the coming seven years, GMO expects a real annual return of minus 2.7 percent on stocks and a return of minus 2.2 percent on bonds—for a 60/40 balanced portfolio, a real return of minus 2.5 percent.

* * *

Gary P. Brinson, CFA, former president of UBS Investment Management, echoes my theme. "For the markets in total, the amount of value added, or alpha, must sum to zero. One person's positive alpha is someone else's negative alpha. Collectively,

(*continued*)

for the institutional, mutual fund, and private banking arenas, the aggregate alpha return will be zero or negative after transaction costs.

"Aggregate fees for the active managers should thus be, at most, the fees associated with passive management. Yet, these fees are several times larger than fees that would be associated with passive management. This illogical conundrum will ultimately have to end."

* * *

Or consider these 2006 words by **Richard M. Ennis, CFA**, Ennis Knupp + Associates, and editor of the *Financial Analysts Journal*: "Today, with interest rates near 4 percent [they're now even lower, about 3 percent] and stocks yielding less than 2 percent, few among us expect double-digit investment returns for any extended period in the near future. Yet, we live with a legacy of that era: historically high fee structures brought on by trillions upon trillions of dollars seeking growth during the boom and shelter in its aftermath. Second, facing the dual challenge of market efficiency and high costs, investors will continue to shift assets from active to passive management. . . . Impetus for this move will be the growing realization that high fees sap the performance potential of even skillful managers."

Chapter Ten

Selecting Long-Term Winners

~

Don't Look for the Needle—Buy the Haystack.

MOST INVESTORS LOOK AT THE disappointing past returns of mutual funds as a group and think, "Sure, but I'll select only good performers!" Sounds easy, but selecting winning funds in advance is more difficult than it looks. Yes, there are always some winners that survive over a quarter-century, but not very many. But if we pore over records of past performance, it is easy to find them.

The mutual funds that we hear the most about are those that have lit up the skies with their glow of past success. We don't hear much about those that did well for a while—even for a long while—and then faltered. And when they falter, they often go out of business—liquidated or merged into other funds. Either way, they vanish, consigned to the dustbin of mutual fund history.

But easy as it is to identify past winners, there is little evidence that such performance persists in the future. Let's first consider the records of funds that have won over the very long term. Exhibit 10.1 goes back to 1970 and shows the 46-year records of the 355 equity funds that existed at the start of that period. The first and most obvious surprise awaits you: *fully 281 of those funds—almost 80 percent—have gone out of business.* If your fund doesn't endure for the long term, how can you invest for the long term?

EXHIBIT 10.1   Winners, Losers, and Failures: Long-Term Returns of Mutual Funds, 1970–2016

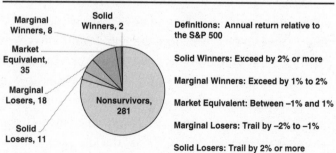

Marginal Winners, 8	Solid Winners, 2
Market Equivalent, 35	Nonsurvivors, 281
Marginal Losers, 18	
Solid Losers, 11	

Definitions: Annual return relative to the S&P 500

Solid Winners: Exceed by 2% or more

Marginal Winners: Exceed by 1% to 2%

Market Equivalent: Between –1% and 1%

Marginal Losers: Trail by –2% to –1%

Solid Losers: Trail by 2% or more

~

A fund failure rate of almost 80 percent.

You can safely assume that it was not the best performers that have gone to their well-earned demise. It was the laggards that disappeared. Sometimes their managers moved on. (The average tenure of active equity fund portfolio managers is just under nine years.) Sometimes giant financial conglomerates acquired their management companies, and the new owners decided to "clean up the product line." (These conglomerates, truth be told, are in business primarily to earn a return on *their* capital as owners of the fund's management company, not on *your* capital as a fund owner.) Often investors fled funds with lagging performance, the funds' assets shrank, and they became a drag on their managers' profits. There are many reasons that funds disappear, few of them good for investors.

But even funds with solid long-term records go out of business. Often, their management companies are acquired by marketing companies whose ambitious executives conclude that, however good the funds' early records, they are not exciting enough to draw huge amounts of capital from new investors. The funds have simply outlived their usefulness. In other cases, experiencing a few years of faltering performance does the job.

---------------- ≈ ----------------

A death in the family.

Sadly, a bit over a decade ago, the second-oldest fund in the entire mutual fund industry was a victim of these attitudes, put out of business by the new owner of its management company. Even though the fund had survived the tempestuous markets of the previous 80 years, it died: *State Street Investment Trust, 1925–2005, R.I.P.* As one of the longest-serving participants in the fund industry, who clearly remembers the classy record of this fund over so many years, I regard the loss of State Street Investment Trust as a death in the family.

---------------- ≈ ----------------

The odds against success are terrible: Only two out of 355 funds have delivered truly superior performance.

In any event, 281 of the equity funds that existed in 1970 are gone, mostly the poor performers. Another 29 remain despite having significantly underperformed the S&P 500 by more than one percentage point per year. Together, then, 310 funds—87 percent of the funds among those original 355—have, one way or another, failed to distinguish themselves. Another 35 funds provided returns within one percentage point, plus or minus, of the return of the S&P 500—market matchers, as it were.

That leaves just 10 mutual funds—*only one fund out of every 35*—that outpaced the market by more than one percentage point per year. Let's face it: *those are terrible odds!* What's more, the margin of superiority of eight of those 10 funds over the S&P 500 was less than two percentage points per year, a superiority that may have been due as much to luck as to skill.

------------------------------ ❧ ------------------------------

The Magellan Fund story.

That still leaves us with two solid long-term winners that outpaced the S&P 500 by more than 2 percentage points per year since 1970. Allow me to salute them: Fidelity Magellan (+2.6 percent per year versus the S&P 500) and Fidelity Contrafund (+2.1 percent).

It is a tremendous accomplishment to outpace the market by more than two percentage points in annual return over almost half a century. Make no mistake about that. But here a curious—perhaps obvious—fact emerges. Let's examine the records of those two funds and see what we can learn.

Exhibit 10.2 charts the growth of Magellan's assets (shaded area) and its return relative to the S&P 500 (black line). As the line rises, Magellan is outperforming the index; as it falls, the index is winning.

Star fund manager Peter Lynch ran Magellan during its heyday (from 1977 through 1990). Since then, five different managers have run the fund as well.[1] But more than manager skill (or luck) is involved here. Magellan's staggering asset growth must also be taken into account.

EXHIBIT 10.2   Fidelity Magellan: Long-Term Record versus S&P 500, 1970–2016

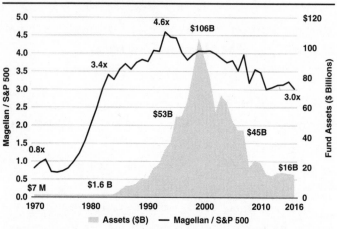

---

[1] As reported in the *Wall Street Journal* on May 28, 2004, Magellan Fund's then-manager Bob Stansky said that "he expects to beat the market by two to five percentage points annually over time. 'I want to win.'" During Mr. Stansky's tenure, Magellan trailed the S&P 500 by 1.2 percent per year. He was replaced in 2005. This is a hard business.

Its greatest gains were achieved shortly after Magellan began with assets of just $7 million. In those early days, the fund outpaced the S&P 500 by an astonishing 10 percent per year (Magellan 18.9 percent, S&P 500 8.9 percent). After the fund's assets passed the $1 billion mark in 1983, the fund's superiority over the market continued, albeit at a lower, yet still impressive rate of 3.5 percent per year (Magellan 18.4 percent, S&P 500 14.9 percent) until the fund's assets hit the $30 billion mark in 1993.

While the fund continued to grow, topping off at a year-end high of $105 billion in 1999, its relative outperformance failed to persist, losing to the S&P 500 by 2.5 percent per year (Magellan 21.1 percent, S&P 500 23.6 percent) from 1994 through 1999.

The fund's underperformance continued after the turn of the century, trailing the S&P 500 by 1.8 percent per year (Magellan 2.7 percent, S&P 500 4.5 percent) even as its assets fell dramatically, from $105 billion in 1999 to $16 billion at the close of 2016, a drop of 85 percent. With money pouring into Magellan when it was "hot" and money pouring out when it turned "cold," this may be the classic case of counterproductive investor behavior.

The Contrafund story.

The Contrafund story, so far, is not dissimilar to Magellan's story during its first 30 years—great success followed by, well, reversion toward the mean. Will Danoff has been the lead portfolio manager since 1990. There's no way to fault his remarkable achievement with Contrafund.

Prior to Danoff taking the reins, the fund outperformed the S&P 500 by 1 percent per year (Contrafund 12.6 percent, S&P 500 11.6 percent). Danoff has nearly tripled that annual advantage during his tenure through 2016 (Contrafund 12.2 percent, S&P 500 9.4 percent). (See Exhibit 10.3.) Yet reversion to the mean always strikes eventually. Over the past five years, Contrafund has

EXHIBIT 10.3   Fidelity Contrafund: Long-Term Record versus S&P 500, 1970–2016

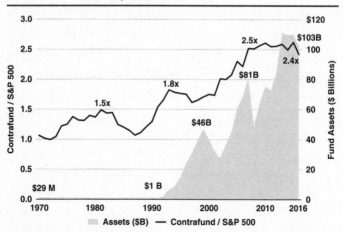

underperformed the S&P 500 by minus 1.2 percent per year (Contrafund 13.5 percent, S&P 500 14.7 percent).

Yet success comes with its challenges. The fund's assets totaled but $300 million when Danoff took over in 1990. In 2013, assets crossed the $100 billion threshold. In the three years since then, Contrafund's superiority has vanished, losing to the index by 1.5 percent per year (Contrafund 12.8 percent, S&P 500 14.3 percent). The future: only time will tell.

When the reported investment returns generated by Magellan and Contrafund were noticed by investors, cash poured in, and they reached giant asset totals. But, as Warren Buffett reminds us, "a fat wallet is the enemy of superior returns." And so it was. As these two popular funds grew, their records turned lackluster. While few actively managed funds will soon reach the mammoth size that Magellan—and even Contrafund—achieved, many, likely most, fund managers will face inflows when times are good and outflows when times are bad, a fundamental challenge to the industry's sensitivity to fluctuating fund returns.

Living by the sword, dying by the sword.

Not all Fidelity funds survived the test of time met by Magellan and Contrafund. One example of failure was Fidelity Capital Fund, formed in 1957 and one of the stars of the Go-Go era. During 1965–1972 its cumulative return totaled 195 percent versus 80 percent for the S&P 500. Yet, in the bear market that followed, the fund fell by 49 percent (the S&P 500 fell by 37 percent). A few years later, its assets down from $727 million in 1967 to $185 million in 1978, it was merged into another Fidelity fund. "If you live by the sword, you die by the sword."

Look (forward) before you leap.

But enough of the past. Let's talk about the future. Before you rush out to invest in Magellan or Contrafund because of their truly remarkable long-term records—outpacing the returns of the S&P 500 by two and a half to three times despite their faltering in later years—think about the next 10 years, or more. Think about the odds that a winning fund will continue to outperform. Think about the fund's present size. Think about the reality that over 25 years the typical fund will replace its managers three times. Think about the likelihood that even a single investor has actually held shares of the fund throughout its lifetime. Think, too, about the odds that a given fund will even *exist* 25 years hence.

Be equally skeptical of any mutual fund that has achieved superior relative returns over a decade or more in the past. It is a changing and competitive world out there in mutual fund land, and no one knows what the future holds. But I wish the very best of luck to the string of portfolio managers who will follow the present manager—and to the shareholders of the funds they run. Whatever you decide, please don't ignore one of the least understood factors that shape mutual fund performance: reversion to the mean. (The remarkable power of RTM will be explored in more detail in the next chapter.)

Don't look for the needle, buy the haystack.

The odds in favor of your owning one of the only two mutual funds (out of 355) with truly superior long-term records were just one-half of 1 percent. However one slices and dices the data, there can be no question that funds with long-serving portfolio managers and records of consistent excellence even over shorter periods are the rare exception rather than the common rule in the mutual fund industry.

The simple fact is that trying to select a mutual fund that will outpace the stock market over the long term is, using Cervantes's formulation, like "looking for a needle in the haystack." So I offer you a cautionary corollary: *"Don't look for the needle in the haystack. Just buy the haystack!"*

The haystack, of course, is the entire stock market portfolio, readily available through a low-cost index fund. The return of a low-cost index fund would have roughly matched or exceeded the returns of 345 of the 355 funds that began the 46-year competition described earlier in this chapter—64 of the 74 funds that survived the long period, plus the 281 funds that failed. I see no reason that such a broad market fund tracking the Standard & Poor's 500 Index cannot achieve a roughly commensurate achievement in the years to come—not through any legerdemain, but merely through the relentless rules of arithmetic that you now must know so well.

∿

Indexing for a lifetime. Two major options: Investing in 30 or 40 active funds and managers, or in one index fund with one non-manager.

Look at it this way: If you're investing for a lifetime, you have two basic options. You can select (as is typical) three or four actively managed funds and hope you select good ones, knowing that their portfolio managers, on average, are likely to last only about nine years, and that the funds themselves are apt to have a life expectancy of little longer than a decade.

Result: You'll own maybe 30 or 40 funds over your lifetime, each carrying that burden of fees and turnover costs. Or (no surprise here) you can invest in a low-fee, minimal-transaction-cost, broad-market index fund, with the certainty that the same non-manager will still closely track its index for the rest of your life. There is really no practicable way that a portfolio of actively managed funds will serve you more effectively and consistently than the index fund. Simplicity, cost efficiency, and staying the course should win the race.

---------------- ∽ ----------------

If you decide against indexing . . .

We know that the index fund will deliver substantially all of the stock market's return. As to the actively managed fund, we know that fund manager changes will inevitably be forthcoming. We know that many of the funds (and, alas, many of their managers) will die. We know that successful funds will draw capital in amounts that are likely to jeopardize their future success. And we accept our inability to be certain how much of a fund's performance is based on luck and how much on skill. In fund performance, the past is rarely prologue.

There is simply no systematic way to assure success by picking the funds that will beat the market, even by looking (perhaps *especially* by looking) to their past performance over the long term. It is like, yes, looking for a needle in a haystack, and with no better odds for finding one.

Don't Take My Word for It

Consider the words of **Warren Buffett** in his 2013 letter to Berkshire Hathaway shareholders as he describes the instructions in his will for managing his wife's trust. Rather than selecting an actively managed mutual fund with a superior record, he directed the trustees to invest 90 percent of the assets in the trust in a "very low-cost S&P 500 index fund. (I suggest Vanguard's.)" It is reasonable to assume that Mr. Buffett considered "looking for the needle." But he finally decided to "buy the haystack."

* * *

Need more advice? With his customary wisdom, the late **Paul Samuelson** summed up the difficulty of selecting superior managers in this parable. "Suppose it was demonstrated that one out of twenty alcoholics could learn to become a moderate social drinker. The experienced clinician would answer, 'Even if true, act as if it were false, for you will never identify that one in twenty, and in the attempt five in twenty will be ruined.' *Investors should forsake the search for such tiny needles in huge haystacks.*"

* * *

In the *Wall Street Journal*, longtime "Getting Going" columnist **Jonathan Clements** asks, "Can you pick the winners?" The answer: "Even fans of actively managed funds often concede that most other investors would be better off in index funds. But buoyed by abundant self-confidence, these folks aren't about to give up on actively managed funds themselves. A tad delusional? I think so. Picking the best-performing funds is 'like trying to predict the dice before you roll them down the craps table,' says an investment adviser in Boca Raton, FL. 'I can't do it. The public can't do it.'

"To build a well-diversified portfolio, you might stash 70 percent of your stock portfolio into

(*continued*)

a [total stock market] index fund and the remaining 30 percent in an international-index fund."

If these comments by a great money manager, a brilliant academic, and a straight-thinking journalist don't persuade you about the hazards of focusing on past returns of mutual funds, just believe what fund organizations tell you. Every single firm in the fund industry acknowledges my conclusion that past fund performance is of no help in projecting the future returns of mutual funds. For in every mutual fund prospectus, in every sales promotional folder, and in every mutual fund advertisement citing a fund's investment returns (albeit often in print almost too small to read), the following warning appears: *"Past performance is no guarantee of future results."* Believe it!

Chapter Eleven

"Reversion to the Mean"

~

Yesterday's Winners, Tomorrow's Losers

IN SELECTING MUTUAL FUNDS, too many fund investors seem to rely less on sustained performance over the very long term (with all of its own profound weaknesses) than on superior performance over the short term. In 2016, over 150 percent of net investor cash flow went to funds rated four or five stars by Morningstar, the statistical service most broadly used by investors in evaluating fund returns.

These "star ratings" are based on a composite of a fund's record over the previous three-, five-, and 10-year periods. (For younger funds, the ratings may cover as few as three years.) As a result, the previous two years' performance alone accounts for 35 percent of the rating of a fund with a 10-year history and 65 percent for a fund in business from three to five years, a heavy bias in favor of recent short-term returns.

How successful are fund choices based on the number of stars awarded for such short-term achievements? Not very! According to a 2014 study by the *Wall Street Journal*, only 14 percent of five-star funds in 2004 still held that rating a decade later. Approximately 36 percent of those original five-star funds dropped one star, and the remaining 50 percent dropped to three or fewer stars. Yes, fund performance reverts toward the mean, or even below.

Reversion to the mean (RTM) is reaffirmed in comprehensive fund industry data.

Other data on fund returns confirm the power of RTM. Consider Exhibit 11.1, comparing the returns of all actively managed U.S. equity funds over two consecutive sets of nonoverlapping five-year periods: 2006–2011 and 2011–2016.

We sorted the returns for each period into quintiles—the top quintile included funds with the best performance, and the bottom quintile contained those with the worst

EXHIBIT 11.1   **Reversion to the Mean, First Five Years 2006–2011 versus Subsequent Five Years 2011–2016**

2006–2011 Ranking			2011–2016 Ranking					
	Number of Funds		Highest Return	High	Medium	Low	Lowest Return	Merged/ Closed
Highest return	353	20%	13%	13%	13%	25%	27%	10%
High	352	20	18	15	14	21	18	12
Medium	353	20	17	17	18	14	16	18
Low	352	20	15	18	20	16	8	22
Lowest return	352	20	17	18	16	10	12	26
Total	1,762	100%	16%	16%	16%	17%	16%	18%

Note: Total number of funds merged or liquidated: 313.

performance. We then looked at how those initial funds fared in the subsequent five-year period.

If it were easy to select funds that would outperform their peers by simply buying yesterday's winners, we would expect to see persistence; that is, most funds that ended the first period at the top of the heap would remain there in the next period and those at the bottom would remain there. But no. As it turns out, RTM overpowers persistence.

Consider the funds that ranked in the top quintile during the first period (2006–2011). Over the subsequent five years, only 13 percent remained in the top quintile. A remarkable 27 percent of the winners from the first period ended up in the bottom quintile, and another 25 percent landed in the next-to-last (fourth) quintile. Even worse, 10 percent of the previous winners didn't even survive the next five years.

At the other end of the spectrum, 17 percent of the first-period laggards ended up at the top of the heap in the subsequent period—even better than the first-period winners! And only 12 percent of the losers repeated their dismal performance in the second period, while 26 percent didn't survive.

You need not be a statistical wizard to observe the remarkable randomness of returns through each of the quintiles, with steady RTM centering around 16 percent in each quintile—less than the 20 percent we started with in the first period. This lower number is because fully 18 percent of the funds from the first period went out of business before the second period ended, presumably due to poor performance.

~

A second study reaffirms the first study—with incredible precision.

You might be wondering if this pattern was just a one-time event, not likely to be repeated. I had the same question. So we looked at the preceding nonoverlapping

EXHIBIT 11.2   Reversion to the Mean, First Five Years 2001–2006 versus Subsequent Five Years 2006–2011

2001–2006 Ranking			2006–2011 Ranking					
	Number of Funds		Highest Return	High	Medium	Low	Lowest Return	Merged/ Closed
Highest return	356	20%	15%	19%	15%	19%	20%	13%
High	355	20	13	15	14	15	23	19
Medium	356	20	14	13	17	17	15	24
Low	355	20	12	16	16	17	10	29
Lowest return	355	20	18	13	12	8	6	43
Total	1,777	100%	14%	15%	15%	15%	15%	26%

Note: Total number of funds merged or liquidated: 454.

five-year period, 2001–2006, and 2006–2011. The pattern held (Exhibit 11.2). Of the top-quintile winners from 2001 to 2006, only 15 percent remained in the top quintile, while 20 percent fell to the bottom. Even worse, 13 percent of the funds—45 funds—failed to survive.

Among the bottom-quintile laggards from 2001 to 2006, 18 percent ended the subsequent period in the top quintile—once again, even better than the first period's winners, only 15 percent of which maintained their position at the top. Only 6 percent of the lowest-ranking funds repeated their dismal performance. 152 of the bottom-quintile funds (43 percent) did not survive.

Just glance over the data in these two exhibits and you will see the recurring pattern of RTM. Like the results in Exhibit 11.1, the second-period results are essentially random. The vast majority of the funds in all five quintiles earned subsequent returns that were largely spread relatively equally over each performance quintile (between 13 percent and 18 percent in each).

From these data, we can conclude that RTM exerts a powerful force on mutual fund returns. There is remarkably little persistence in returns among the top and bottom funds alike. I don't amaze easily. But these data are truly amazing. They dramatically belie the assumption of most investors and advisers that manager skill will persist. Most investors seem to believe that manager skill will persist. But it doesn't. *We are "fooled by randomness."*[1]

———————————— ∾ ————————————

The stars produced in the mutual fund field rarely remain stars; all too often they become meteors.

————————————————————————————————————

The message is clear: reversion to the mean (RTM)— the tendency of funds whose records substantially exceed industry norms to return toward the average or below—is alive and well in the mutual fund industry. In stock market blow-offs, "the first shall be last." But in more typical environments, reversion to the fund mean is the rule. So please remember that the stars produced in the mutual fund field

—————————
[1] The title of a provocative book by Nassim Nicholas Taleb.

are rarely stars; all too often they are meteors, lighting up the firmament for a brief moment in time and then flaming out, their ashes floating gently to earth.

With each passing year, the reality is increasingly clear: relative returns of mutual funds are random. Yes, there are rare cases where skill seems to be involved, but it would require decades to determine how much of a fund's success can be attributed to luck, and how much attributed to skill.

If you disagree and decide to invest in a fund with superior recent performance, you might ask yourself questions like these: (1) How long will the fund manager, with the same staff and with the same strategy, remain on the job? (2) If the fund's assets grow many times larger, will the same results that were achieved when the fund was small be sustained when it is large? (3) To what extent did high expense ratios and/or high portfolio turnover detract from the fund's performance, or did low expenses and low turnover enhance performance? (4) Will the stock market continue to favor the same kinds of stocks that have been at the heart of the manager's style?

———————————— ∾ ————————————

**Picking winning funds based on past performance
is hazardous duty.**

In short, selecting mutual funds on the basis of recent performance is all too likely to be hazardous duty, and it is almost always destined to produce returns that fall far short of those achieved by the stock market, itself so easily achievable through an index fund.

It might help our understanding if we each ask ourselves just why it is so hard to recognize the powerful principle of reversion to the mean that punctuates not only mutual funds' returns, but almost every corner of our lives. In his 2013 book *Thinking, Fast and Slow*, here's how Nobel laureate Daniel Kahneman answered that question.

> [O]ur mind is strongly biased toward causal explanations and does not deal well with "mere statistics." When our attention is called to an event, associative memory will look for its cause . . . but they [causal explanations] will be wrong because the truth is that regression to the mean has an explanation but does not have a cause.

Don't Take My Word for It

As this book was about to go to press, *The Economist* commentator **Buttonwood** struck almost precisely the same note as this chapter:

"Suppose you had picked one of the best-performing 25 percent of American equity mutual funds in the 12 months, to March 2013. In the subsequent 12 months, to March 2014, only 25.6 percent of those funds stayed in the top quartile. That result is no better than chance. In the subsequent 12-month periods, this elite bunch is winnowed down to 4.1 percent, 0.5 percent, and 0.3 percent—all figures that are worse than chance would predict. Similar results apply if you had picked one of the best-performing 50 percent of all funds; those in the upper half of the charts failed to stay there.

"Suppose you had picked a fund with a top-quartile performance in the five years to March 2012. What proportion of those funds would be in the top quartile over the subsequent five years (to March 2017)?

"The answer is just 22.4 percent: again, less than chance would suggest. Indeed, 27.6 percent of the star funds in the five years to March 2012 were in the worst-performing quartile in the five years to March 2017. Investors had a higher chance of picking a dud than a winner."

The old saying that "past performance is no guide to the future" is not a piece of compliance jargon. It is the math.

(continued)

* * *

Listen to **Nassim Nicholas Taleb**, author of *Fooled by Randomness*: "Toss a coin; *heads* and the manager will make $10,000 over the year, *tails* and he will lose $10,000. We run [the contest] for the first year [for 10,000 managers]. At the end of the year, we expect 5,000 managers to be up $10,000 each, and 5,000 to be down $10,000. Now we run the game a second year. Again, we can expect 2,500 managers to be up two years in a row; another year, 1,250; a fourth one, 625; a fifth, 313.

"We have now, simply in a fair game, 313 managers who made money for five years in a row. [In 10 years, just 10 of the original 10,000 managers—only 0.1 percent—will have tossed heads in each year.] Out of pure luck . . . a population entirely composed of bad managers will produce a small amount of great track records. . . . The number of managers with great track records in a given market depends far more on the number of people who started in the investment business (in place of going to dental school), rather than on their ability to produce profits."

* * *

That may sound theoretical, so here is a practical outlook. Hear *Money* magazine's colloquy with

Ted Aronson, partner of respected Philadelphia investment management firm AJO:

Q. You've said that investing in an actively managed fund (as opposed to a passively run index fund) is an act of faith. What do you mean?

A. Under normal circumstances, it takes between 20 and 800 years [of monitoring performance] to statistically prove that a money manager is skillful, not lucky. To be 95 percent certain that a manager is not just lucky, it can easily take nearly a millennium—which is a lot more than most people have in mind when they say "long-term." Even to be only 75 percent sure he's skillful, you'd generally have to track a manager's performance for between 16 and 115 years. . . . Investors need to know how the money management business really works. It's a stacked deck. The game is unfair.

Q. Where do you invest?

A. In Vanguard index funds. I've owned Vanguard Index 500 for 23 years. Once you throw in taxes, it just skewers the argument for active management. Personally, I think indexing wins hands-down. After tax, active management just can't win.

(continued)

* * *

Finally, *Wall Street Journal* columnist and author **Jason Zweig** sums up performance chasing in a single pungent sentence: "Buying funds based purely on their past performance is one of the stupidest things an investor can do."

Chapter Twelve

Seeking Advice to Select Funds?

Look Before You Leap.

———————— ∽ ————————

THE EVIDENCE PRESENTED IN Chapters 10 and 11 teaches two lessons: (1) Selecting winning equity funds over the long term offers all the potential success of finding a needle in a haystack. (2) Selecting winning funds based on their performance over relatively short-term periods in the past is all too likely to lead, if not to disaster, at least to disappointment.

So why not abandon these "do-it-yourself" approaches, and rely on professional advice? Pick a financial consultant (the designation usually given to the stockbrokers of Wall

Street, and indeed brokers everywhere); or a registered investment adviser (RIA, the designation usually applied to nonbrokers, who often—but not always—work on a "fee-only" basis rather than on a commission basis); or even an insurance agent offering investment "products" such as variable annuities. (Beware!)

Registered investment advisers (RIAs) can play a vital role in providing investors with assistance.

In this chapter, I'll attempt to answer the question about the value of investment consultants. You'll note that I'm skeptical of the ability of advisers as a group to help you select equity funds that can produce superior returns for your portfolio. (Some do. Most do not.)

Professional investment advisers are best at providing other valuable services, including asset allocation guidance, information on tax considerations, and advice on how much to save while you work and how much to spend when you retire. Further, most advisers are always there to consult with you about the financial markets.

Advisers can encourage you to prepare for the future. They can help you deal with many extra-investment decisions that have investment implications (for example, when you want to build a fund for your children's college education or need to raise cash for the purchase of a home). Experienced advisers can help you avoid the potholes along the investment highway. (Put more grossly, they can help you to avoid making such dumb mistakes as chasing past performance, or trying to time the market, or ignoring fund costs.) At their best, these important services can enhance the implementation of your investment program and improve your returns.

A large majority of investors rely on brokers or advisers for help in penetrating the dense fog of complexity that, for better or worse, permeates our financial system. If the generally accepted estimate that some 70 percent of the 55 million American families who invest in mutual funds do so through intermediaries is correct, then about 15 million families choose the "do-it-yourself" road. The remaining 40 million families rely on professional helpers for investment decision making. (That's essentially the unsuccessful strategy described in my opening parable about the Gotrocks family's Helpers.)

Helpers—adding value or subtracting value?

We'll never know exactly how much value is added—or subtracted—by these Helpers in selecting mutual funds for your portfolio. But it's hard for me to imagine that as a group they are other than, well, average (before their fees are taken into account). That is, their advice on equity fund selection produces returns for their clients that are probably not measurably different from those of the average fund, and therefore several percentage points per year behind the stock market, as measured by the S&P 500 Index. (See Chapter 4.)

However, I'm willing to consider the possibility that the fund selections recommended by investment advisers (RIAs and brokers) may be better than average. As I explained in Chapter 5, if they merely select funds with the lowest all-in costs—hardly rocket science—they'll do better for you. If they're savvy enough to realize that high-turnover funds are tax-inefficient, they'll pick up important additional savings for you in transaction costs and taxes. If you put those two policies together and emphasize low-cost index funds—as so many advisers do—so much the better for the client.

If you can avoid jumping on the bandwagon . . .

And if professional investment consultants are wise enough—or lucky enough—to keep their clients from jumping on the latest and hottest bandwagon (for example, the tech-stock craze of the late 1990s, reflected in the mania for funds investing in "new economy" stocks), their clients may earn returns that easily surpass the disappointing returns achieved by fund investors as a group. Remember the additional shortfall of about one and one-half percentage points per year relative to the average equity fund that we estimated in Chapter 7? To remind you, the average nominal investor return came to just 6.3 percent per year during 1991–2016, despite a strong stock market in which a simple S&P 500 Index fund earned an annual return of 9.1 percent.

Alas (from the standpoint of the advisers), there is simply no evidence that the fund selection advice RIAs and brokers provide has produced any better returns than those achieved by fund investors on average. In fact, the evidence goes the other way. A study by a research team led by two Harvard Business School professors concluded that between 1996 and 2002, "the underperformance of broker-channel funds (funds managed by the salesman's employer) relative to funds sold through the direct channel (purchased directly by investors) cost investors approximately $9 billion per year."

Average annual return of funds recommended by advisers: 2.9 percent. For equity funds purchased directly: 6.6 percent.

Specifically, the study found that broker and adviser asset allocations were no better, that they chased market trends, and that the investors they advised paid higher up-front charges. The study's conclusion: *The weighted average return of equity funds held by investors who relied on advisers (excluding all charges paid up front or at the time of redemption) averaged just 2.9 percent per year, compared with 6.6 percent earned by investors who took charge of their own affairs.*

This powerful evidence, however, does not bring the researchers to the clear conclusion that advice in its totality has negative value: "We remain," the report states, "open to the possibility that substantial intangible benefits exist, and will undertake more research to identify these intangible benefits and explore the elite group of advisers who do improve the welfare of households who trust them."

The Merrill Lynch debacle: a case study.

There is even more powerful evidence that the use of stockbrokers (as distinct from RIAs) has a strong negative impact on the returns earned by fund investors. In a study prepared for Fidelity Investments covering the 10-year period 1994 to 2003 inclusive, broker-managed funds had the lowest ratings relative to their peers of any group of funds. (The other groups included funds operated by privately owned managers, by publicly owned managers, by managers owned by financial conglomerates, and by bank managers.)

In the Fidelity study, the Merrill Lynch funds were 18 percentage points (!) below the fund industry average. The Goldman Sachs and Morgan Stanley funds were 9 percentage points below average. Both the Wells Fargo and Smith Barney funds were 8 percentage points behind in terms of 10-year returns.

Part of the reason for this performance failure may arise from the nature of the job. The brokerage firm and its brokers/financial consultants must sell something every single day. If they don't they won't survive. When a brokerage firm introduces a new fund, the brokers have to sell it to someone. (Imagine a day when nobody sold anything, and the stock market lay fallow, silent all day long.)

Two terrible ideas: the Focus Twenty fund and the Internet Strategies fund.

This powerful example illustrates the Merrill Lynch debacle, a shocking example of the destructive challenges that may be faced by investors who rely on stockbrokers. In March 2000, just as the bubble created by the Internet stock craze reached its peak, Merrill Lynch, the world's largest stock brokerage firm, jumped on the bandwagon with two new funds to sell. One was a "Focus Twenty" fund (based on the then-popular theory that if a manager's 100 favorite stocks were good, surely his 20 favorites would be even better). The other was an "Internet Strategies" fund.

The public offering of the two funds was an incredible *success*. Merrill's brokers pulled in $2.0 billion from their trusting (or was it performance chasing?) clients, $0.9 billion in Focus Twenty, and $1.1 billion in Internet Strategies.

A marketing success for Merrill Lynch, an investment failure for its clients.

The subsequent returns of the funds, however, were an incredible *failure*. (This was not surprising. The best time to *sell* a new fund to investors—when it's hot—is often the worst time to *buy* it.) Internet Strategies tanked almost immediately. Its asset value dropped 61 percent during the remainder of 2000 and another 62 percent by October 2001. The total loss for the period was a cool 86 percent.

Most of the fund's investors cashed out their shares at staggering losses. When the fund's original $1.1 billion of assets had plummeted to just $128 million, Merrill decided to kill Internet Strategies and give it a decent burial, merging it with another Merrill fund. (Keeping a record like that alive would have been a continuing embarrassment to the firm.)

Investment disaster: Clients lose 80 percent of their assets.

For what it's worth, the losses in Focus Twenty were less severe. Its asset value declined 28 percent in the remainder of 2000, another 70 percent in 2001, and another 39 percent in 2002, before finally posting positive returns in the three years that followed. On balance, its cumulative lifetime return through late 2006 came to minus 79 percent. Investors have regularly withdrawn their capital, and the fund's assets, which had reached almost $1.5 billion in 2000, currently languish at $82 million, a 95 percent decline. Unlike its Internet Strategies cousin, Focus Twenty soldiers on, now known as BlackRock Focus Growth. The lesson remains: The $2 billion marketing success of the Merrill Lynch Internet Strategies fund and Focus Twenty fund resulted in an investment disaster for

Merrill's clients, who lost some 80 percent of their hard-earned savings.

The value of financial consultants.

Despite their disappointing results (as a group) and that example of colossal failure by brokerage firm Merrill Lynch, RIAs can add value to investors in many other ways. I endorse the idea that for many—indeed, most—investors, financial advisers may provide valuable services in helping to give you peace of mind; in helping you establish a sensible portfolio that matches your appetite for reward and your tolerance for risk; in helping you deal with the complexities, nuances, and tax implications of investing in mutual funds; and in helping you stay the course in troubled seas. But the evidence I've presented so far strongly confirms my original hypothesis that, as vital as those services may be, advisers as a group cannot be credibly relied upon to add value by selecting funds that will beat the market.

The rise of the robo-adviser.

In recent years, a new method of providing advice to investors has developed. A number of new firms have taken advantage of record-keeping technology and offered computerized "robo-advice" directly to investors, often with little or no face-to-face interaction.

These firms claim the advantage of tax-loss harvesting, but otherwise generally have recommended buy-and-hold portfolios with asset allocation among bond and stock index funds. They typically focus on exchange-traded index funds, with their ready liquidity and absence of limits on frequent transactions often imposed by fund managers.

The growth of robo-advisers has been rapid. In 2017, the two pioneering robo-advisers report about $10 billion of client assets under management. But so far robo-advisers represent only a tiny fraction of total investor assets served by RIAs. With annual fees that are extremely low (often around 0.25 percent), they may well become a significant participant in the field of advice going forward.

------------------------------- ∼ -------------------------------

Simplicity beats complexity.

Despite being dated or anecdotal, the evidence in this chapter is an eye-opener to the challenge faced by complex investment strategies. In all, this evidence suggests that, yet again, the simplicity of a broad-market, low-cost index fund, bought and then held forever, is likely to be the optimal strategy for the vast majority of investors.

If you are considering the selection of an RIA, a stockbroker, or an insurance agent to provide you with investment advice, please take heed of these findings. If you decide to go ahead, make sure you are paying a fair fee, for fees paid to advisers result in a significant deduction from whatever rate of return your fund portfolio earns. Since most investment advisory fees tend to begin in the range of 1 percent per year and then scale down, be sure to balance the worth of the peripheral services that advisers provide against the reduction in your returns that those fees are likely to represent over time. Finally—and this will hardly surprise you—look with particular favor on advisers who recommend stock and bond index funds in their model portfolios.

The fiduciary standard.

I close this chapter with good news for clients who rely on professional advice in selecting and managing their mutual fund portfolios. There is a developing trend toward establishing a federal standard of fiduciary duty for advisers. This means, simply put, that advisers are required to place your interests first. The standard approved in 2016 by the Department of Labor would apply only to firms and persons offering retirement plans to investors, such as individual retirement accounts (IRAs), 401(k) thrift plans, and 403(b) thrift plans. RIAs are already held to a fiduciary standard for all of their clients under existing law, but the application of the standard to stockbrokers and insurance agents represents a major extension to the principle, "put the client first."

Ultimately the new standard must be expanded to encompass not only retirement plans but *all* accounts of *all* clients. Yet even now, a partisan political move is afoot to dilute or eliminate the existing standard, set to become effective in 2017. But the reality is that, even if the present proposal ultimately fails, the principle of fiduciary duty—of putting the client first—will prevail. The arc of investment is long, but it bends toward fiduciary duty.

Don't Take My Word for It

Listen to the widely respected investment adviser **William Bernstein**, who wrote these words in his book *The Four Pillars of Investment Wisdom*: "You

(continued)

will want to ensure that your adviser is choosing your investments purely on their investment merit and not on the basis of how the vehicles reward him.

"The warning signs here are recommendations of load funds, insurance products, limited partnerships, or separate accounts. The best, and only, way to make sure that you and your adviser are on the same team is to make sure that he is 'fee-only,' that is, that he receives no remuneration from any other source besides you. . . .

"'Fee-only' is not without pitfalls, however. Your adviser's fees should be reasonable. It is simply not worth paying anybody more than 1 percent to manage your money. Above $1 million, you should be paying no more than 0.75 percent, and above $5 million, no more than 0.5 percent. . . .

"Your adviser should use index/passive stock funds wherever possible. If he tells you that he is able to find managers who can beat the indexes, he is fooling both you and himself. I refer to a commitment to passive indexing as 'asset-class religion.' Don't hire anyone without it."

Chapter Thirteen

Profit from the Majesty of Simplicity and Parsimony

———— ∼ ————

*Hold Traditional Low-Cost Index Funds
That Track the Stock Market.*

WHAT LESSONS HAVE WE learned in the previous chapters?

- Costs matter (Chapters 5, 6, and 7).
- Selecting equity funds based on their long-term past performance doesn't work (Chapter 10).
- Fund returns revert to the mean (RTM) (Chapter 11).
- Relying even on the best-intentioned advice works only sporadically (Chapter 12).

If low costs are good (and I don't think a single analyst, academic, or industry expert would disagree with the idea that low costs are good), why wouldn't it be logical to focus on the lowest-cost funds of all—traditional index funds (TIFs) that own the entire stock market? Some of the largest TIFs carry annual expense ratios as low as 0.04 percent, and incur turnover costs that approach zero. Their all-in costs, then, can come to just four basis points per year, 96 percent below even the 91 basis points for the *lowest-cost* quartile of funds described in Chapter 5.

And it works. Witness the real-world superiority of the S&P 500 Index fund compared with the average equity fund over the past 25 years and over the previous decade, as described in earlier chapters. The case for the success of indexing in the past is compelling and unarguable. And with the outlook for subdued returns on stocks during the decade ahead, let's conclude our anecdotal stroll through the relentless rules of humble arithmetic with a final statistical example that suggests what the future may hold.

------------------------------ ∿ ------------------------------

The Monte Carlo simulation.

We can, in fact, use statistics designed to project the odds that a passively managed index fund will outpace an actively managed equity fund over various time periods. The complex exercise is called a "Monte Carlo simulation."[1] What it does is make a few simple assumptions about the volatility of equity fund returns and the extent to which they vary from the returns earned in the stock market, as well as an assumption about the all-in costs of equity investing. The particular example presented here assumes that index fund costs will run to 0.25 percent per year and that the all-in costs of active management will run to 2 percent per year. (Index funds are available at far lower costs, and many equity funds carry even higher costs. So we've given actively managed funds the benefit of a very large doubt.)

Result: Over one year, about 29 percent of active managers, on average, would be expected to outpace the index, and over five years about 15 percent would. After 50, years only 2 percent of active managers would be expected to win (Exhibit 13.1).

~

The majesty of simplicity in an empire of parsimony.

---

[1] A common Monte Carlo simulation technique takes all the monthly returns earned by stocks over a long period (even a full century), scrambles them randomly, and then computes the annual rates of return generated by each of the thousands of hypothetical portfolios.

EXHIBIT 13.1   Odds of an Actively Managed Portfolio Outperforming Passive Index Fund

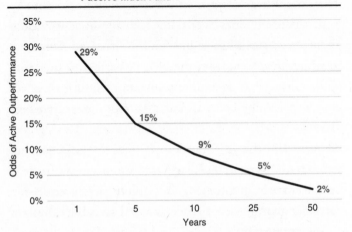

How will the future actually play out? Of course, we can't be sure. But we know what the past 25 years looked like, and we saw in Chapter 10 that since 1970 only two of the 355 funds in business at the outset outperformed the stock market index by 2 percent or more per year. What's more, one of these winners lost its early edge two full decades ago. So it looks as if our statistical odds are in the right ballpark. This arithmetic suggests—even demands—that index funds deserve an important place in your portfolio, even as they constitute the overriding portion of my own portfolio.

In the era of subdued stock and bond market returns that most likely lies in prospect, fund costs will become more important than ever—even more so when we move from the illusion that mutual funds as a group can capture whatever returns our financial markets provide to the even greater illusion that most mutual fund investors can capture even those depleted returns in their own fund portfolios. What the index fund has going for it is, as I have often said, "the majesty of simplicity in an empire of parsimony."

To reiterate: all those pesky costs—fund expense ratios, sales charges, turnover costs, tax costs, and the most subtle cost of all, the rising cost of living (inflation)—are virtually guaranteed to erode the real spending power of our investments over time. What's more, only in the rarest cases do fund investors actually succeed in capturing the returns that the funds report.

$\sim$

My conclusions rely on mathematical facts—the relentless rules of humble arithmetic.

My conclusions about the market returns that we can expect in the years ahead may be wrong—too high or too low. But my conclusions about the share of those returns that funds will capture, and the share of those returns that we investors will actually enjoy, have one thing in common:

They rely, not on opinion, but largely on mathematical facts—*the relentless rules of humble arithmetic*—that make selecting winning funds akin to looking for a needle in a haystack. Ignore these rules at your peril.

If the road to investment success is filled with dangerous turns and giant potholes, never forget that simple arithmetic can enable you to moderate those turns and avoid those potholes. So do your best to diversify to the nth degree, minimize your investment expenses, and focus your emotions where they cannot wreak the kind of havoc that most other investors experience. Rely on your own common sense. Emphasize an S&P 500 Index fund or an all-stock-market index fund. (They're pretty much the same.) Carefully consider your risk tolerance and the portion of your investments you allocate to equities. Then, stay the course.

All index funds are not created equal. Costs to investors vary widely.

I should add, importantly, that all index funds are not created equal. Although their index-based portfolios are substantially identical, their costs are anything but identical. Some have minuscule expense ratios; others have expense ratios that surpass the bounds of reason. Some are no-load funds, but nearly a third, as it turns out, have substantial front-end loads, often with an option to pay those loads over a period of (usually) five years; others entail the payment of a standard brokerage commission.

The gap between the expense ratios charged by the low-cost funds and the high-cost funds offered by 10 major fund organizations for their S&P 500 Index–based funds runs upward of an amazing 1.3 percent of assets per year (Exhibit 13.2). Worse, the high-cost index funds also saddle investors with front-end sales loads.

EXHIBIT 13.2   Costs of Selected S&P 500 Index Funds

Five Low-Cost 500 Index Funds	Annual Expense Ratio	Sales Load
Vanguard 500 Index Admiral	0.04%	0.0%
Fidelity 500 Index Premium	0.045	0.0
Schwab S&P 500 Index	0.09	0.0
Northern Stock Index	0.10	0.0
T. Rowe Price Equity Index 500	0.25	0.0
Five High-Cost Funds		
Invesco S&P 500 Index	0.59%	1.10%
State Farm S&P 500 Index	0.66	1.00
Wells Fargo Index	0.45	1.15
State Street Equity 500 Index	0.51	1.05
JPMorgan Equity Index	0.45	4.80

Even among the low-cost S&P 500 Index funds, we see a wide range of expenses. While the Admiral class of Vanguard's index fund carries a minuscule 0.04 percent expense ratio, the T. Rowe Price fund charges 0.25 percent. Although lower than the high-cost index funds, that T. Rowe Price fund is hardly "low." Assuming an annual return of 6 percent compounded over 25 years, an initial investment of $10,000 would grow to $40,458 in the T. Rowe Price index fund. With a truly low-cost index fund carrying an expense ratio of 0.04 percent, that $10,000 investment would grow to $42,516, an increase of $2,058 over the higher-cost index fund. Yes, even seemingly small differences in costs matter.

Today, there are some 40 traditional index mutual funds designed to track the S&P 500 Index, 14 of which carry front-end loads ranging between 1.5 percent and 5.75 percent. The wise investor will select only those index funds that are available without sales loads, and those operating with the lowest costs. These costs—no surprise here!— directly relate to the net returns delivered to the shareholders of these funds.

— ∽ —

Two funds. One index. Different costs.

The first index fund was created by Vanguard in 1975. It took nine years before the second index fund appeared— Wells Fargo Equity Index Fund, formed in January 1984. Its subsequent return can be compared with that of the original Vanguard 500 Index Fund since then.

Both funds selected the S&P 500 Index as their benchmark. The sales commission on the Vanguard Index 500 Fund was eliminated within months of its initial offering, and it now operates with an expense ratio of 0.04 percent (4 basis points) for investors who have $10,000 or more invested in the fund.

In contrast, the Wells Fargo fund carried an initial sales charge of 5.5 percent, and its expense ratio averaged 0.80 percent per year (the current expense ratio is 0.45 percent). Behind the eight-ball at the start, the fund falls further behind with each passing year.

∼

Your index fund should not be your manager's cash cow. It should be your own cash cow.

During the 33 years since 1984, these seemingly small differences added up to a 27 percent enhancement in value for the Vanguard fund. An original investment of $10,000 grew to $294,900 in the Vanguard 500 Index Fund as 2017 began, compared with $232,100 for the Wells Fargo Equity Index Fund. *All index funds are not created equal.* Intelligent investors will select the lowest-cost index funds that are available from reputable fund organizations.

Some years ago, a Wells Fargo representative was asked how the firm could justify such high charges. The answer: "You don't understand. It's our cash cow." (That is, it regularly generates lots of profits for the manager.) By carefully selecting the lowest-cost index funds for your portfolio, you can be sure that the fund is not the manager's cash cow, but your own.

Whether markets are efficient or not, indexing works.

Conventional wisdom holds that indexing may make sense in highly efficient corners of the market, such as the S&P 500 for large-cap U.S. stocks, but that active management may have an advantage in other corners of the market, like small-cap stocks or non-U.S. markets. That allegation turns out to be false.

As shown in Exhibit 3.3 in Chapter 3, indexing works perfectly well wherever it has been implemented. *As it must.* For, whether markets are efficient or inefficient, all investors as a group in that segment earn the return of that segment. In inefficient markets, the most successful managers may achieve unusually large returns—but that means some other manager suffered unusually large losses. Never forget that, as a group, all investors in any discrete segment of the stock market must be, and are, average.

————————————— ∾ —————————————

International funds also trail their benchmark indexes.

International funds are also subject to the same allegation that it is easier for managers to win in (supposedly) less efficient markets. But to no avail. S&P reports that its international index (world markets, less U.S. stocks) outpaced 89 percent of actively managed international equity funds over the past 15 years.

Similarly, the S&P emerging markets index outpaced 90 percent of emerging market funds. With indexing so successful in both more efficient and less efficient markets alike, and in U.S. markets and global markets, I'm not sure what additional data would be required to close the case in favor of index funds of all types.

~

Caution about gambling.

Caution: While investing in particular market sectors is done most efficiently through index funds, betting on one winning sector and then another is exactly that: betting. *But betting is a loser's game.*

Why? Largely because emotions are almost certain to have a powerful negative impact on the returns that investors achieve. Whatever returns each sector may earn, the returns of investors in those very sectors will likely, if not certainly, fall well behind them. There is abundant evidence that the most popular sector funds of the day are those that have recently enjoyed the most spectacular recent performance. As a result, a strategy of trading based on after-the-fact popularity is a recipe for unsuccessful investing.

When trying to pick which market sector to bet on, look before you leap. It may not be as exciting as gambling, but owning the traditional stock market index fund at rock-bottom cost is the ultimate strategy. It holds the mathematical certainty that marks it as the gold standard in investing. Try as they might, the alchemists of active management cannot turn their own lead, copper, or iron into gold. Avoid complexity and rely on simplicity and parsimony, and your investments should flourish.

Don't Take My Word for It

You may think that I am too pessimistic in calculating the odds that only 2 percent of all equity mutual portfolios will outperform the stock market over 50 years. If so, consider the odds calculated by **Michael J. Mauboussin**, chief market strategist at Credit Suisse, adjunct professor at Columbia Business School, and author of the best-selling *More Than You Know*. While my 2 percent estimate would mean that 1 portfolio in 50 would outperform the stock market over 50 years, Mauboussin calculates the odds of a fund outperforming for 15 years consecutively at 1 in 223,000, and at 1 in 31 million over 21 years. Either way, the odds of outpacing an all-market index fund are, well, terrible.

* * *

Now listen to Warren Buffett's widely esteemed Berkshire Hathaway partner **Charlie Munger**, who eloquently states the case for shunning the foolish complexity of investing and instead opting for simplicity: "At large charitable foundations in recent years there has been a drift toward more complexity. In some endowment funds, there

(continued)

are not few but many investment counselors, chosen by an additional layer of consultants who are hired to decide which investment counselors are best, help in allocating funds to various categories, insure that claimed investment styles are scrupulously followed . . . [plus] a third layer of the security analysts employed by investment banks.

"There is one thing sure about all this complexity: the total cost of all the investment management, plus the frictional costs of fairly often getting in and out of many large investment positions, can easily reach 3 percent of foundation net worth per annum. All the equity investors, in total, will surely bear a performance disadvantage per annum equal to the total croupiers' costs they have jointly elected to bear. . . .

"It is unescapable that exactly half of the investors will get a result below the median result after the croupier's take, a median result that may well be somewhere between unexciting and lousy. The wiser choice is to dispense with the consultants and reduce the investment turnover, by changing to indexed investment in equities." (Once again, shades of the Gotrocks family.)

Chapter Fourteen

Bond Funds

~

Where Those Relentless Rules of Humble Arithmetic Also Prevail.

SO FAR, MY APPLICATION of common sense has been applied largely to the stock market, to equity mutual funds, and to equity index funds. But the relentless rules of humble arithmetic with which I've regaled you also apply—arguably even more forcefully—to bond funds.

Perhaps it's obvious why this is so. While a seemingly infinite number of factors influence the stock market and each individual stock that is traded there, a single factor dominates the returns earned by investors in the bond market: the prevailing level of interest rates.

Managers of fixed-income funds can't do much, if anything, to influence rates. If they don't like the rates established in the marketplace, neither calling the Treasury Department or the Federal Reserve, nor otherwise trying to change the supply/demand equation, is likely to bear fruit.

———————————— ∾ ————————————

Why would an intelligent investor hold bonds?

Over the long term, history tells us that stocks have generally provided higher returns than bonds. That relationship is expected to continue during the coming decade, although rational expectations suggest that future returns both on stocks and on bonds are almost certain to fall well short of historical norms.

As noted in Chapter 9, I estimate that annual returns on bonds over the coming decade will average 3.1 percent. To summarize, since 1900, annual returns on bonds have averaged 5.3 percent; since 1974, 8.0 percent; in the coming decade, likely 3.1 percent, plus or minus.

So today, why would an intelligent investor hold any bonds at all? First, because the long run is a series of short runs, and during many short periods, bonds have provided higher returns than stocks. In the 117 years since 1900, bonds have outpaced stocks in 42 years; in the 112 five-year periods, bonds have outpaced stocks 29 times; and even in the 103 fifteen-year periods, bonds have outpaced stocks 13 times.

Second, and perhaps more important, reducing the volatility of your portfolio can give you downside protection during large market declines, an anchor to windward, so to speak. The conservative nature of a balanced stock/bond portfolio can reduce the possibility of counterproductive investor behavior (i.e., getting frightened when the stock market plunges and liquidating your stock position).

Third, while bond yields are near their lowest levels since the early 1960s, the current yield on bonds (3.1 percent) still exceeds the dividend yield on stocks (2 percent).

A similar gap between bond yields and stock yields.

In fact, that positive yield spread of 1.1 percentage points for bonds over stocks is remarkably close to the 1.4 percentage point yield advantage held by bonds during the recent era (since 1974, 6.9 percent average yield on bonds, 5.5 percent average yield on stocks). So even in this era of low interest rates (and low dividend yields), bonds remain relatively competitive.

Given these considerations, the question then becomes, not "Why should I own bonds?," but "What portion of my portfolio should be allocated to bonds?" We'll tackle that question in Chapter 18.

Bond fund managers track the bond market.

As a group, managers of bond funds will almost inevitably deliver a gross return that parallels the baseline constituted by the current interest rate environment. Yes, a few managers might do better—even do better for a long while—by being extra smart, or extra lucky, or by taking extra risk.

Alas, bad decisions often come home to roost, and can impair longer-term returns. (Reversion to the mean often strikes.) What's more, even if bond managers add a few fractions of 1 percent to the funds' gross returns, they rarely overcome the fund expenses, fees, and sales loads involved in acquiring their services.

Bonds vary in riskiness.

While these costs make the task of improving returns far more difficult, overly confident bond fund managers may be tempted to take just a little extra risk by extending maturities of the bonds in the portfolio. (Long-dated bonds—with, say, 30-year maturities—are much more volatile than short-term bonds—say, two years—but usually provide higher yields.)

Managers also may be tempted to increase returns by reducing the investment quality of the portfolio, holding less in U.S. Treasury bonds (rated AA+) or in investment-grade corporate bonds (rated BBB or better), and holding more in below-investment-grade bonds (BB or lower), or even some so-called junk bonds, rated below CC or even unrated. Heavy reliance on junk bonds to increase the income generated by your portfolio subjects your bond investment to high risks. (Of course!) Investors who seek to increase the yield on their bond portfolios by investing in junk bond funds should limit themselves to small allocations. Caution is advised!

---------------- ≈ ----------------

Three basic types of bond funds.

One beneficial feature of bond mutual funds is that they often offer investors three (or more) options that deal with the trade-off between return and risk. Short-term portfolios are designed for investors who are willing to sacrifice yield to reduce volatility risk. Long-term portfolios serve investors who want to maximize yield and are prepared to deal with higher volatility. And intermediate-term portfolios seek a balance between income opportunity and market volatility. These options help make bond funds attractive to investors with a variety of strategies.

------------------------------ ∼ ------------------------------

Like stock funds, actively managed bond funds lag their benchmarks. Why? The arithmetic of costs.

When all is said and done, bond funds of comparable maturity and credit quality are likely to capture the gross returns of the bond market segments dictated by their policies. And after their expense ratios, operating costs, and sales loads (if any) are deducted, their net returns will fall short. Where bonds are concerned, Brandeis's warning becomes particularly meaningful: *"Remember, O Stranger, arithmetic is the first of the sciences and the mother of safety."*

There are too many types of bond funds to try your patience by examining the performance of all of them. So I'll now focus on funds in the three major maturity segments (short-, intermediate-, and long-term bonds), and two major quality segments (U.S. government and investment-grade corporate bonds).

In Chapter 3, I noted that the returns of 90 percent of actively managed equity mutual funds lagged their benchmark indexes, as reported by S&P in its SPIVA (Standard and Poor's Indices versus Active) report.

The SPIVA report also compares the returns of bond mutual funds in various categories to their appropriate benchmark indexes. During the 15-year period from 2001 to 2016, the performance of the bond indexes is also impressive, outpacing an average of 85 percent of all actively managed bond funds in the six categories—short-term, intermediate-term, and long-term bond funds grouped by both U.S. government and investment grade corporate sectors (Exhibit 14.1). The appropriate indexes also outperformed the managers of municipal bond funds (84 percent) and high-yield bond funds (96 percent).

～

The important role of costs in shaping bond fund returns.

EXHIBIT 14.1   Percentage of Actively Managed Bond Funds Outperformed by S&P Indexes, 2001–2016

Fund Category	U.S. Government	Investment Grade
Short-term bonds	86%	73%
Intermediate-term bonds	82	73
Long-term bonds	97	97
Average	88%	81%

The average shortfall in the returns of intermediate-term and short-term Treasury and corporate bond funds relative to index funds during the past 15 years is estimated by SPIVA to be about 0.55 percent per year. The average bond index fund carried annual costs of about 0.10 percent, while the expense ratio for actively managed bond funds averaged 0.75 percent. The average difference in expense ratios came to about 0.65 percent, slightly larger than the performance gap. Once again, it is clear that low costs account for a dominant portion of the index advantage.

The total bond market index fund.

The first total bond market index fund—formed in 1986, and still the largest—tracks the Bloomberg Barclays U.S. Aggregate Bond Index. Nearly all of the major all-bond-market index funds have followed the leader. These index funds are extremely high in quality (63 percent U.S. government-backed bonds, another 5 percent in AAA-rated corporates, 32 percent rated AA through BAA, and no bonds rated below investment grade). During the past 10 years, that total bond market index fund earned an annual return of 4.41 percent, just 0.05 percentage points behind the 4.46 percent annual return of its target index, a remarkable parallel.

Since high-quality portfolios almost always produce lower yields than lower-quality portfolios, the total bond market index fund's yield in mid-2017 is a relatively low 2.5 percent when compared to the 3.1 percent yield of the bond market proxy that we used earlier in this chapter. The difference: the bond portfolio that we constructed for this analysis underweights U.S. government issues (50 percent) and overweights investment-grade corporate bonds (50 percent) relative to the index, thus producing its higher yield.

In order to achieve such a 50/50 government/corporate bond portfolio, investors who require a higher yield than the total bond market index fund (yet still seek a high-quality portfolio) might consider a portfolio consisting of 75 percent in the total bond market index fund and 25 percent in an investment-grade corporate bond index fund.

The value of bond index funds is created by the same forces that create value for stock index funds.

The reality is that the value of bond index funds is derived from the same forces that create value in stock index funds: broad diversification, rock-bottom costs, disciplined portfolio activity, tax efficiency, and focus on shareholders who place their trust in long-term strategies.

It is these commonsense characteristics that enable index funds to guarantee that you will earn your fair share of the returns in the stock and bond markets, even as they do in all financial markets.

Indeed, many of the earlier chapters in this book that were focused on stock funds could just as easily be the titles of a series of bond fund chapters—especially, "Focus on the Lowest-Cost Funds," "Selecting Long-Term Winners," and "Profit from the Majesty of Simplicity and Parsimony." These rules are universal.

Don't Take My Word for It

The power of bond indexing is growing. **Peter Fisher**, former head of the fixed-income group at giant global money manager BlackRock, has observed: "We're moving to the second phase of the index revolution. The world is a frightening, uncertain place, and investors want to make their [bond] portfolios much simpler so they can sleep at night."

* * *

While not a lot has been written about the remarkable (and remarkably obvious) value of index funds that invest in bonds, the convictions expressed in this chapter have been strongly reinforced by **Walter R. Good, CFA**, and **Roy W. Hermansen, CFA**, in *Index Your Way to Investment Success*. "Comparison of expenses, transaction costs, and, where applicable, sales loads identify the cost advantage for bond index funds.... For the actively managed load funds, the index fund advantage amounts to 1.2 percentage points per year.

"The data provide a sobering glimpse of the challenge encountered by the active bond fund manager ... and suggest how much additional return active management may have to add—on average over an extended period—just to break even!"

* * *

Further confirmation comes from across the pond. England's **Tim Hale**, author of *Smarter Investing: Simpler Decisions for Better Results*, writes, "You should not overlook the efficacy of index investing for bonds, which up to now has been whispered rather than shouted from the rooftops. The evidence is compelling and comes down firmly in favour of investing in index

(continued)

funds. . . . Over the 10-year period 1988–1998, U.S. bond index funds returned 8.9 per cent a year against 8.2 per cent for actively managed bond funds . . . [with] index funds beating 85 per cent of all active funds. This differential is largely due to fees."

Chapter Fifteen

The Exchange-Traded Fund (ETF)

A Trader to the Cause?

DURING THE PAST DECADE, the principles of the traditional index fund (TIF) have been challenged by a sort of wolf in sheep's clothing, the exchange-traded fund (ETF). Simply put, the ETF is an index fund designed to facilitate trading in its shares, dressed in the guise of the traditional index fund.

If long-term investment was the paradigm for the original TIF designed 42 years ago, surely using index funds as trading vehicles can only be described as short-term speculation. If the broadest possible diversification was the original paradigm, surely holding discrete—even widely diversified—sectors of the market offers far less diversification and commensurately more risk. If the original paradigm was minimal cost, then this is obviated by holding market-sector index funds that carry higher costs, entail brokerage commissions when they are traded, and incur tax burdens if one has the good fortune to trade successfully.

But let me be clear. There is nothing wrong with investing in those indexed ETFs that track the broad stock market, *just so long as you don't trade them*. While short-term speculation is a loser's game, long-term investment is a proven strategy, one that broad market index funds are well positioned to implement.

ETF traders have absolutely no idea what relationship their investment returns will bear to the returns earned in the stock market.

The quintessential aspect of the original paradigm of the TIF is to assure, indeed virtually guarantee, that investors will earn their fair share of the stock market's return. ETF traders, however, have nothing remotely resembling such a guarantee. In fact, after all of the selection challenges, timing risks, extra costs, and added taxes, ETF traders can have absolutely no idea what relationship their

THE EXCHANGE-TRADED FUND (ETF)   [181]

EXHIBIT 15.1 Traditional Index Funds versus Exchange-Traded Index Funds

	TIFs	ETFs Broad Index Funds Investing	ETFs Broad Index Funds Trading	Specialized Index Funds
Broadest possible diversification	Yes	Yes	Yes	No
Longest time horizon	Yes	Yes	No	Rarely
Lowest possible cost	Yes	Yes	Yes*	Yes*
Greatest possible tax efficiency	Yes	Yes	No	No
Highest possible share of market return	Yes	Yes	Unknown	Unknown

*But only if trading costs are ignored.

investment returns will bear to the returns earned in the stock market.

These differences between the *traditional* index fund—the TIF—and the index fund *nouveau* represented by the ETF are stark (Exhibit 15.1). Exchange-traded funds march to a different drummer than the original index fund. In the words of the old song, I'm left to wonder, "What have they done to my song, ma?"

───────── ∾ ─────────

The creation of the "Spider."

The first U.S. exchange-traded fund, created in 1993 by Nathan Most, was named "Standard & Poor's Depositary Receipts" (SPDRs), and quickly dubbed the "Spider." It was a brilliant idea. Investing in the S&P 500 Index, operated at low cost with high tax efficiency, priced in real time but held for the long term, it held the prospect of providing ferocious competition to the traditional S&P 500 Index fund.[1] (Brokerage commissions, however, made it less suitable for investors making small investments regularly.)

The Spider 500 remains the largest ETF, with assets of more than $240 billion in early 2017. During 2016, some 26 billion shares of the Spider S&P 500 were traded, a total dollar volume of an amazing $5.5 trillion, and an annual turnover rate of 2,900 percent. In terms of dollar volume, every day the Spider was the most widely traded stock in the world.

Spiders and other similar ETFs are primarily used by short-term investors. The largest users, holding about one-half of all ETF assets, are banks, active money managers, hedgers, and professional traders, who trade their ETF shares with a frenzy. These large traders turned over their holdings at an average rate of nearly 1,000 percent(!) in 2016.

---

[1] The late Mr. Most, a fine man, initially offered to partner with Vanguard, using our S&P 500 Index fund as the trading vehicle. Since I see trading as a loser's game for investors and a winner's game for brokers, I declined his offer. But we parted friends.

—— ⁓ ——

ETF growth explodes.

From that single S&P 500 ETF, ETFs have grown to account for fully half of the asset base of all index funds—as 2017 began, $2.5 trillion of the $5 trillion total. That 50 percent market share is up from 41 percent in 2007 and only 9 percent in 1997.

ETFs have become a force to be reckoned with in the financial markets. The dollar volume of their trading sometimes constitutes as much as 40 percent or more of the total daily trading volume on the entire U.S. stock market. ETFs have proved to meet the needs of investors and speculators alike, but they have also proved to be manna from heaven for stockbrokers.

The amazing growth of ETFs certainly says something about the energy of Wall Street's financial entrepreneurs, about the focus of money managers on gathering assets, about the marketing power of brokerage firms, and about the willingness—nay, eagerness—of investors to favor complex strategies and aggressive trading, continuing to believe, against all odds, that they can beat the market. We shall see.

—— ⁓ ——

The ETF stampede.

The growth of ETFs has approached a stampede, not only in number but in diversity. There are now more than 2,000 ETFs available (up from 340 a decade ago), and the range of investment choices available is remarkable.[2]

The profile of ETF offerings differs radically from the profile of TIF offerings (Exhibit 15.2). For example, only 32 percent of ETF assets are invested in broadly diversified stock market index funds (U.S. and international) such as the Spider, compared to fully 62 percent of TIF assets. There are 950 ETFs offering concentrated, speculative, inverse, and leveraged strategies holding 23 percent of ETF assets. But there are only 137 such TIFs (holding 5 percent of TIF assets).

There are also 669 ETFs focused on smart beta and factor strategies, 244 based on stock market sectors, and 156 concentrating their assets in particular foreign countries. There are also 196 broad-based bond ETFs and 422 utilizing high leverage (enabling speculators to bet on the stock market's direction and then double, triple, or even quadruple daily swings in the stock market!), tracking commodity prices and currencies, and using other high-risk strategies.

---

[2] As of this writing, some 250 more ETFs have been launched in the past 12 months, and some 200 have gone out of business. The high rate of ETF launches and closures suggests a new investment fad. Such fads have rarely enhanced the well-being of investors.

EXHIBIT 15.2 Composition of TIF Assets and ETF Assets, December 2016

	Traditional Index Funds (TIFs)			
	Assets (Billions)		Number of Funds	
Diversified U.S. stock	$1,295	47%	67	16%
Diversified non-U.S. stock	421	15	43	10
Diversified bonds	489	18	50	12
Factor/smart beta	423	15	129	30
Concentrated/speculative	132	5	137	32
Total	$2,760	100%	426	100%

	Exchange-Traded Funds (ETFs)			
	Assets (Billions)		Number of Funds	
Diversified U.S. stock	$477	20%	40	2%
Diversified non-U.S. stock	287	12	94	5
Diversified bonds	355	15	196	10
Factor/smart beta	756	31	669	34
Concentrated/speculative	562	23	950	49
Total	$2,438	100%	1,949	100%

What is more, investor cash flows into ETFs are exceptionally volatile, especially when compared to the relatively stable cash flows experienced by TIFs. During the 24 months from the stock market high in April 2007 to April 2009 (shortly after the low of the 50 percent market crash), TIFs experienced *not a single month* of negative flows. Flows into ETFs, however, were negative in 10 of the 24 months, ranging from inflows of $31 billion in December 2007 (near the market's high) to outflows of $18 billion in February 2009, when stock prices hit bottom. Counterproductive investor behavior writ large.

Yes, in almost every respect, most ETFs have strayed far from the concepts of buy-and-hold, diversification, and rock-bottom cost that are exemplified by the traditional index fund.

The renowned Purdey shotgun is great for big-game hunting in Africa. It's also an excellent weapon for suicide.

Broad-market ETFs constitute the only instance in which an ETF can replicate, and possibly even improve on, the five paradigms listed earlier for the original index fund—*but only when they are bought and held for the long term.* Their annual expense ratios tend to be comparable to their TIF counterparts, although their transaction commissions erode the returns that investors earn.

The early advertisements for the Spider claimed, *"Now you can trade the S&P 500 all day long, in real time."* And so you can. But to what avail? I can't help likening the ETF—a cleverly designed financial instrument—to the renowned Purdey shotgun, supposedly the world's best.

The Purdey may be great for big-game hunting in Africa. But it's also an excellent weapon for suicide. I suspect that too many ETFs will prove, if not suicidal to their owners in financial terms, at least wealth-depleting.

———————— ∼ ————————

The temptation to chase past returns.

But whatever returns each sector ETF may earn, the investors in those narrow ETFs will likely, if not certainly, earn returns that fall well behind them. There is abundant evidence that the most popular sector funds of the day are those that have recently enjoyed the most spectacular recent performance. But such success does not endure. (Again, remember reversion to the mean [RTM].)

In fact, such after-the-fact popularity is a recipe for unsuccessful investing. That was the lesson of Chapter 7—that mutual fund investors almost always do significantly worse than the funds they own, and do still worse when they choose funds that are less diversified and more volatile. That pattern is likely to be repeated, even magnified, in ETFs.

Among the 20 best-performing ETFs, for 19 funds, investor returns fell short of ETF returns.

To illustrate this point, consider the records of the 20 best-performing ETFs during 2003–2006. Only one ETF earned a better return for its shareholders than the return reported by the ETF itself. The average short-fall in shareholder returns was equal to 5 percentage points per year, with the largest gap fully 14 percentage points (iShares Austria reported a return of 42 percent, but its investors earned just 28 percent).

"HANDLE WITH CARE" should be the first warning on the ETF label, though I have yet to see it used. Or perhaps: "CAUTION: Performance Chasing at Work."

THE EXCHANGE-TRADED FUND (ETF)

A "double whammy": betting on hot
market sectors (emotions) and paying
heavy costs (expenses) are sure to be hazardous
to your wealth.

And so we have a "double whammy." Investors who choose, or are persuaded by their brokers, to actively trade ETFs face the near-inevitability of counterproductive market timing, as investors bet on sectors as they grow hot—and bet against them when they grow cold. Second, those heavy commissions and fees accumulate over time, as expenses take a growing toll on ETF returns.

Together, these two enemies of the equity investor— emotions and expenses—are sure to be hazardous to your wealth, to say nothing of consuming giant globs of time that you could easily use in more productive and enjoyable ways.

Beginning in 2006, ETFs became the cutting edge of the alleged "market-beating" strategies that I'll describe in the next chapter. The entrepreneurs and marketers of these so-called smart beta strategies seem to believe that their "fundamental indexing" and "factor" approaches are winning long-term strategies. Yet by choosing the ETF format, they strongly imply that bringing stockbrokers into the distribution mix—and encouraging investors to actively buy and sell their ETFs—will lead to even larger short-term profits. I doubt it.

ETFs are a dream come true for entrepreneurs and brokers. But are they an investor's dream come true?

ETFs are clearly a dream come true for entrepreneurs, stockbrokers, and fund managers. But is it too much to ask whether these exchange-traded index funds are an investor's dream come true? Do investors really benefit from being able to trade ETFs "all day long, in real time"? Is less diversification better than more diversification?

Is trend following a winner's game or a loser's game? Are ETFs truly low-cost vehicles after we add their brokerage commissions and taxes on short-term profits to their expense ratios? Is buy-and-sell (often with great frequency) really a better strategy than buy-and-hold?

Finally, if the traditional index fund was designed to capitalize on the wisdom of long-term investing, aren't investors in these exchange-traded index funds too often engaging in the folly of short-term speculation?

Doesn't your own common sense give you the answers to these questions?

The interests of the business versus the interests of the clients.

On the broad spectrum that lies between advancing the interests of those in the investment business and the interests of their clients, where do ETFs fit? If you are making a single large initial purchase of either of those two versions of classic indexing—the Vanguard 500 ETF or the Spider 500 ETF—at a low commission rate and holding the shares for the long term, you'll profit from the broad diversification and the low expense ratios that both offer. You may even enjoy a bit of extra tax efficiency from these broad market ETFs.

But if you trade these two ETFs, you're defying the relentless rules of humble arithmetic that are the key to successful investing. And if you like the idea of sector ETFs, invest in the appropriate ones, and don't trade them.

Answering my question.

Let me now answer the question I asked at the outset of this chapter, "What have they done to my song, ma?" As the creator of the world's first traditional index fund all those years ago, as I observe the ETF phenomenon I can only answer: "They've tied it up in a plastic bag and turned it upside down, ma; that's what they've done to my song."

In short, the ETF is a *trader to the cause* of the TIF. I urge intelligent investors to stay the course with the proven index strategy. While I can't assure you that traditional index investing is the best strategy ever devised, I can assure you that the number of strategies that are worse is infinite.

Don't Take My Word for It

In an essay entitled "Indexing Goes Hollywood," here's what **Don Phillips**, managing director of Morningstar, has said: "[T]here is a dark side to indexing that investors should not ignore. The potential for harm to investors increases as index offerings become more specialized, which is exactly what has happened in the world of ETFs. . . . In the right hands, precision tools can create great things; in the wrong ones, however, they can do considerable damage.

"In creating more complex offerings, the index community has found new revenue sources from . . . very specialized tools, but it has done so at the risk of doing considerable harm to less sophisticated investors. The test of character facing the index community is whether it ignores that risk or steps up and tries to mitigate it. The continued good name of indexing lies in the balance."

* * *

From **Jim Wiandt**, founder of ETF.com (ironically, formerly named IndexUniverse.com): "I have always found it ironic that indexing—like almost everything else in the world of finance—comes in waves. Hedge fund indexes, microcap indexes, dividend indexes, commodities indexes, China indexes, and 'enhanced' indexes are all flavors of the month. And I'll give you three guesses as to what all these indexes have in common: (1) chasing returns, (2) chasing returns, or (3) chasing returns.

"If you believe in indexing, then you know that there is no free money. Ultimately, the push toward enhanced indexing is about enhancing the

(continued)

bottom line for managers. . . . But it's important for us to keep our eyes on the ball and remember what makes indexing, well, indexing: low fees, broad diversification, hold, hold, hold. Don't believe the hype. Try to beat the market—in any manner—and you're likely to get beaten . . . by about the cost of doing it."

* * *

And now listen carefully to the candid warnings from two senior officers of a major ETF sponsor. **Chief executive:** "For most people, sector funds don't make a lot of sense. . . . [Don't] stray too far from the market's course." **Chief investment officer:** "It would be unfortunate if people focused pinpoint bets on very narrowly defined ETFs. These still involve nearly as much risk as concentrating on individual stock picks. . . . You're taking extraordinary risk. It's possible to take a good thing too far. . . . *How many people really need them?*"

Chapter Sixteen

Index Funds That Promise to Beat the Market

The New Paradigm?

SINCE THE INCEPTION OF the first index mutual fund in 1975, traditional index funds (TIFs) designed for the long-term investor have proved to be both a remarkable artistic success and an incredible commercial success.

In previous chapters, we've demonstrated—pretty much unequivocally—the success of index funds in providing long-term returns to investors that have vastly surpassed the returns achieved by investors in actively managed mutual funds.

Given that artistic success, the commercial success of indexing is hardly surprising. (Although it was a long time coming!) The principles of the original S&P 500 Index model have stood the test of time. Today, the lion's share of the assets of TIFs are those that track the broad U.S. stock market (the S&P 500 or the total stock market index), the broad international stock market, and the broad U.S. bond market.

Assets of these traditional stock index funds have soared from $16 million in 1976 to $2 trillion in early 2017—20 percent of the assets of all equity mutual funds. Assets of traditional bond index funds have also soared— from $132 million in 1986 to $407 billion in 2017— 13 percent of the assets of all taxable bond funds. Since 2009, TIF assets have grown at an 18 percent annual rate, slightly faster than their ETF cousins.

Success breeds competition.

In many arenas, indexing has become a competitive field. The largest managers of TIFs are engaged in fiercely competitive price wars, cutting their expense ratios to draw the assets of investors who are smart enough to real-ize that costs make the difference.

This trend is great for index fund investors. But it slashes the profits of index fund managers and discourages entrepreneurs who start new fund ventures in the hopes of enriching themselves by building fund empires.[1]

─────────────── ∿ ───────────────

Passive ETF strategies designed to outpace stock market returns.

───────────────────────────────────────

How, then, have index fund promoters taken advantage of the proven attributes that underlie the success of the TIF? Why, they create new indexes and join the exchange-traded fund (ETF) parade! Then, they claim (or at least strongly imply) that their new index strategies will consistently outpace the broad market indexes that up until now have pretty much defined how we think about indexing.

ETF managers charge a higher fee for that higher potential reward, whether or not it is ever actually delivered (usually not). Offering the promise of earning excess returns, a whole host of ETFs have sprung up to entice investors and speculators alike.

─────────────── ∿ ───────────────

Active managers versus active strategies.

───────────────────────────────────────

─────────────

[1] The Vanguard funds operate on an at-cost basis, so it is largely economies of scale rather than competition that reduce the expenses borne by its index fund shareholders.

Let's consider the difference between the approaches of traditional active money managers and the approach of ETF managers. Active managers know that the only way to beat the market portfolio is to depart from the market portfolio. And this is what active managers strive to do, individually.

Collectively, they can't succeed. For their trading merely shifts ownership from one holder to another. All of that swapping of stock certificates back and forth, however it may work out for a given buyer or seller, in the aggregate it enriches only our financial intermediaries.

But active managers have a vested financial interest in making the case that if they have done well in the past, they will continue to do so in the future. And if they haven't done well in the past, well, better days are always ahead.

Sponsors of ETFs, on the other hand, make no claim to prescience. Rather, most rely on one of these two strategies: (1) Offer broad market index funds that investors can profitably trade in real time. (This seems to be a specious claim.) (2) Create indexes for a wide range of narrow market sectors that investors can swap back and forth, earning extra profits. (In fact, the evidence goes the other way.)

So what's happening is that the responsibility for investment management and portfolio strategy is being shifted from active fund *managers* to active mutual fund *investors*. This crucial shift has broad implications for Main Street investors. I confess to being skeptical that this change will serve investors well.

—————————— ∾ ——————————
**The new breed of passive indexers are
active strategists.**
————————————————————————

The new breed of passive indexers have largely chosen the ETF structure to market their products. It's an easy market to enter. In recent years, "smart beta" ETFs (whatever exactly that means) have become a hot product.

Smart beta managers create their own indexes—not, in fact, indexes in the traditional sense, but active strategies claiming to be indexes. They focus on weighting portfolios by so-called factors—stocks with similar forces driving their returns. Rather than weighting portfolio holdings by their market capitalizations, they may focus on a single factor (value, momentum, size, etc.) or they may use a combination of factors such as corporate revenues, cash flows, profits, and dividends. One smart beta ETF portfolio, for example, is weighted by the dollar amount of dividends distributed by each corporation, rather than weighted by the market capitalizations of its components.

—————————— ∾ ——————————
**Not a terrible idea, but not a world-changing
one, either.**
————————————————————————

As a concept, smart beta is not a terrible idea, nor is it a world-changing one. Smart beta ETF managers rely on computers to parse heavily mined past data on stocks that will enable fund managers to identify factors that can be easily packaged as ETFs. The goal is to create great profits for the manager by gathering the assets of investors seeking a performance edge.

Mark me as from Missouri on these strategies. Of course it seems easy. But it isn't. Consistently outpacing the market is difficult, in part because of the power of reversion to the mean in mutual fund returns. Today's winning factors are all too likely to be tomorrow's losing factors. Investors who disregard RTM are all too likely making a huge mistake.

"Remembrance of things past."

With the rise of ETFs, once again remember the "Go-Go" fund craze of 1965–1968 and the "Nifty Fifty" craze of 1970–1973; popular fads are driving product creation in the fund industry. These products are great for fund sponsors, but almost always awful for fund investors. Let me remind you of this time-honored principle: *Successful short-term marketing strategies are rarely—if ever—optimal long-term investment strategies.*

And this will not surprise you—the fundamental factors that ETF entrepreneurs typically identify as the basis for their portfolio strategies have actually outpaced the traditional indexes in the past. (We call this *data mining*. You can be sure that no one would have the temerity to promote a new strategy that has lagged the traditional index fund in the past.) But in investing, the past is rarely prologue to the future.

Recent events confirm skepticism about the power of smart beta.

Nonetheless, the assets of these smart beta ETFs (renamed "strategic beta" by Morningstar) have ballooned—from $100 billion in 2006 to more than $750 billion currently. They have accounted for a remarkable 26 percent of mutual fund industry cash flows during the first four months of 2017.

At the same time, the two major strategic beta styles—value and growth—have done a U-turn. During 2016, the value index rose 16.9 percent, while the growth index provided a far smaller 6.2 percent gain. But so far in 2017 (through April) the growth index has leaped by 12.2 percent, while the value index has struggled to earn a 3.3 percent gain. Yes, both are short periods to evaluate factor strategies. But, perhaps unsurprisingly, it seems that RTM has struck once again.

──────────── ∽ ────────────

"The new Copernicans"?

The members of this new breed of smart beta ETF indexers are not shy about their prescience. They claim variously, if a tad grandiosely, that they represent a "new wave" in indexing, a "revolution" that will offer investors a "new paradigm"—a combination of higher returns and lower risk.

Indeed, the believers in factor-based indexes have described themselves as "the new Copernicans," after the sixteenth-century astronomer who concluded that the center of our solar system was not the earth, but the sun. They compared traditional market-cap-weighted indexers with ancient astronomers who attempted to perpetuate the Ptolemaic view of an Earth-centered universe. And they assured the world that we're at the brink of a "huge paradigm shift" in indexing. Over the past decade, smart beta has represented a small paradigm shift. But even its earliest advocate, the so-called "godfather of smart beta," recently described a smart beta crash as "reasonably likely." (I doubt it.)

------------------------------ ❧ ------------------------------

Let's look at the record.

Over the past decade, both the original "fundamental" index fund and the first "dividend-weighted" index fund have had the opportunity to prove the value of their theories. What have they proven? Essentially *nothing*. Exhibit 16.1 presents the comparisons.

You'll note that the fundamental index fund earned higher returns while assuming higher risk than the S&P 500 fund. The dividend index, on the other hand, earned lower returns and carried lower risk. But when we calculate the risk-adjusted Sharpe ratio, the S&P 500 Index fund wins in both comparisons.

The similarity of returns and risks in all three funds should not be surprising. Each holds a diversified portfolio

EXHIBIT 16.1   "Smart Beta" Returns: 10-Year Period Ended December 31, 2016

	Fundamental Index Fund	Dividend Index Fund	S&P 500 Index Fund
Annual return	7.6%	6.6%	6.9%
Risk (standard veviation)	17.7	15.1	15.3
Sharpe ratio*	0.39	0.38	0.40
Correlation with S&P 500 Index	0.97	0.97	1.00

*A measure of risk-adjusted return.

with similar stocks—simply weighted differently. In fact, given the remarkably high correlation of 0.97 of both smart beta ETFs with the returns earned by the S&P 500, both could easily be classified as high-priced "closet index funds."

What the S&P 500 index portfolio offers is the certainty that its investors will earn nearly the entire return of the stock market index. These two smart beta ETFs may also do that. We just don't know. You must ask yourself these questions: "Among similar portfolios, do I prefer a certain (relative) outcome or an uncertain one? Is it better to be safe than sorry?" Only you can decide.

When an active manager of an equity fund claims to have a way of uncovering extra value in our highly (but not perfectly) efficient U.S. stock market, investors will look at the past record, consider the strategies, and invest or not. Many of these new smart beta ETF managers are in fact active managers. But they not only claim prescience, but a prescience that gives them confidence that certain sectors of the market (such as dividend-paying stocks) will outperform the broad index as far ahead as the eye can see. That thesis defies reason—and the lessons of history.

———————————— ~ ————————————

"The greatest enemy of a good plan is the dream of a perfect plan." Stick to the good plan.

Traditional market-cap-weighted index funds (such as the Standard & Poor's 500) guarantee that you will receive your fair share of stock market returns, and virtually assure that you will outperform, over the long term, at least 90 percent of the other investors in the marketplace. Maybe this new paradigm of factor indexing—unlike all the other new paradigms that I've seen—will work. But maybe it won't.

I urge you not to be tempted by the siren song of paradigms that promise the accumulation of wealth that are far beyond the rewards of the traditional index fund. Don't forget the prophetic warning of Carl von Clausewitz, military theorist and Prussian general of the early nineteenth century: *"The greatest enemy of a good plan is the dream of a perfect plan."* Put your dreaming away, pull out your common sense, and stick to the good plan represented by the traditional index fund.

Don't Take My Word for It

I feel strongly on this point. But I am not alone. First hear these words from **Gregory Mankiw**, Harvard professor and former chairman of the President's Council of Economic Advisers during

(continued)

the George W. Bush administration, speaking about the competition between traditional index funds and smart beta. "I am placing my bets with Bogle on this one." (He was right.)

* * *

Then listen to **William Sharpe**, professor of finance at Stanford University and Nobel laureate in economics: "Smart beta is stupid. . . . It is quite remarkable that people think that somehow a scheme that weights stocks differently than capitalization can dominate a capitalization-weighted index. . . . New paradigms come and go. Betting against the market (and spending a considerable amount of money to do so) is indeed likely to be a hazardous undertaking."

* * *

Finally, consider this affirmation of traditional indexing from Wharton School professor **Jeremy Siegel**, author of *Stocks for the Long Run* and adviser to WisdomTree Investments, the promoter of the dividend-driven factor model. "It can be shown that maximum diversification is achieved by holding each stock *in proportion to its value to the entire market* [italics added]. . . . Hindsight plays tricks on our minds ... often distorts the past and encourages us to play hunches and out-guess other investors, who in turn are playing the same game. For most of us, trying to beat the market leads to disastrous results ... our actions lead to much lower returns than can be achieved by just staying in the market ... matching the market year after year with index funds [such as] the Vanguard 500 Portfolio ... and Vanguard's Total Stock Market Index Fund." (This quotation is from the first edition of Dr. Siegel's book in 1994. I understand that he has every right to change his mind.)

Chapter Seventeen

What Would Benjamin Graham Have Thought about Indexing?

~

*Mr. Buffett Confirms Mr. Graham's
Endorsement of the Index Fund.*

THE FIRST EDITION OF *The Intelligent Investor* was published in 1949. It was written by Benjamin Graham, the most respected money manager of his era. *The Intelligent Investor* is regarded as the best book of its kind—comprehensive, analytical, perceptive, and forthright—a book for the ages.

Although Benjamin Graham is best known for his focus on the kind of value investing represented by the category of stocks he described as "bargain issues," he cautioned, "the aggressive investor must have a considerable knowledge of security values—enough, in fact, to warrant viewing his security operations as equivalent to a business enterprise . . . armed with mental weapons that distinguish him from the trading public. It follows from this reasoning that *the majority of security owners should elect the defensive classification.*"

Investors should be satisfied with the reasonably good return obtainable from a defensive portfolio.

Why? Because "[the majority of investors] do not have the time, or the determination, or the mental equipment to embark upon such investing as a quasi-business. They should therefore be satisfied with the reasonably good return obtainable from a defensive portfolio, and they should stoutly resist the recurrent temptation to increase this return by deviating into other paths."

The first index mutual fund was not formed until 1974, a quarter-century after *The Intelligent Investor* was published in 1949. But Graham was presciently describing the essence of that precedent-setting fund. (Coincidently, it was also in 1949 that an article in *Fortune* magazine introduced me to the mutual fund industry, inspiring me to write my 1951 Princeton senior thesis on mutual funds. There, I first hinted at the index fund idea: "[Mutual funds] can make no claim to superiority over the market averages.")

For the defensive investor who required assistance, Graham originally recommended professional investment advisers who rely on "normal investment experience for their results . . . and who make no claim to being brilliant [but] pride themselves on being careful, conservative, and competent . . . whose chief value to their clients is in shielding them from costly mistakes."

Graham cautioned investors not to expect too much from stock-exchange houses, arguing that "the Wall Street business fraternity . . . is still feeling its way toward the high standards and standing of a profession." (A half-century later, the quest remains far from complete.)

Wall Street—"a Falstaffian joke."

He also noted, profoundly if obviously, that Wall Street is "in business to make commissions, and that the way to succeed in business is to give customers what they want, trying hard to make money in a field where they are condemned almost by mathematical law to lose." Later on, in 1976, Graham described his opinion of Wall Street as "highly unfavorable . . . a Falstaffian joke that frequently degenerates into a madhouse . . . a huge laundry in which institutions take in large blocks of each other's washing." (Shades of the ideas of two of the top managers of university endowment funds, Jack Meyer, formerly of Harvard, and David Swensen of Yale, both of whom we heard from earlier.)

In that first edition of *The Intelligent Investor*, Graham commended the use by investors of leading investment funds as an alternative to creating their own portfolios. Graham described the well-established mutual funds of his era as "competently managed, making fewer mistakes than the typical small investor," carrying a reasonable expense, and performing a sound function by acquiring and holding an adequately diversified list of common stocks.

The truth about mutual fund managers.

Graham was bluntly realistic about what fund managers might accomplish. He illustrated this point in his book with data showing that from 1937 through 1947, when the Standard & Poor's 500 Index provided a total return of 57 percent, the average mutual fund produced a total return of 54 percent, excluding the oppressive impact of sales loads. (The more things change, the more they remain the same.)

Graham's conclusion: "The figures are not very impressive in *either* direction . . . on the whole, the managerial ability of invested funds has been just about able to absorb the expense burden and the drag of uninvested cash." In 1949, however, fund expenses and turnover costs were, remarkably, far lower than in the modern fund industry. That change helps explain why, as fund returns were overwhelmed by these costs in recent decades, the figures were impressive in a negative rather than a positive direction.

~

"Unsoundly managed funds can produce spectacular but largely illusionary profits for a while, followed inevitably by calamitous losses."

By 1965, Graham's confidence that funds would produce the market's return, less costs, was shaken. "Unsoundly managed funds," he noted in the 1973 edition of *The Intelligent Investor*, "can produce spectacular but largely illusionary profits for a while, followed inevitably by calamitous losses." He was describing the so-called per-formance funds of the mid-1960s Go-Go era, in which a "new breed that had a spectacular knack for coming up with winners . . . [funds managed by] bright, ener-getic, young people who promised to perform miracles with other people's money . . . [but] who have inevitably brought losses to their public in the end."

Graham could have as easily been presciently describ-ing the hundreds of risky "new economy" mutual funds formed during the great technology-stock-driven bull market of the late 1990s, and the utter collapse in their asset values, far worse than the 50 percent market crash that followed. (See Exhibit 7.2 in Chapter 7.)

~

"The real money in investment will have to be made . . . not out of buying and selling but of owning and holding securities . . . [for their] dividends and benefitting from their long-term increase in value."

Graham's timeless lessons for the intelligent investor are as valid today as when he prescribed them in his first edition. Benjamin Graham's timeless message:

> The real money in investment will have to be made—as most of it has been made in the past—not out of buying

and selling but of owning and holding securities, receiving interest and dividends and benefitting from their long-term increase in value.

Graham's philosophy has been reflected over and over again in this book, best exemplified in the parable of the Gotrocks family in Chapter 1 and the distinction between the real market of corporate intrinsic value and the expectations market of ephemeral stock prices described in Chapter 2.

------------------------------ ∾ ------------------------------

The Graham 1949 strategy—precursor to the 1976 index fund.

Owning and holding a diversified list of securities? Wouldn't Graham recommend a fund that essentially buys the entire stock market and holds it forever, patiently receiving interest and dividends and increases in value? Doesn't his admonition to "strictly adhere to *standard, conservative,* and even *unimaginative* forms of investment" eerily echo the concept of the stock market index fund? When he advises the defensive investor "to emphasize diversification more than individual selection," has not Benjamin Graham come within inches of describing the modern-day stock index fund?

~

The failure of investment managers.

Late in his life, in an interview published in 1976, Graham candidly acknowledged the inevitable failure of individual investment managers to outpace the market. Coincidentally, the interview took place at almost the very moment in August 1976 when the public offering of the world's first mutual index fund—First Index Investment Trust, now Vanguard 500 Index Fund—was taking place.

The interviewer asked Graham, "Can the average manager obtain better results than the Standard & Poor's Index over the years?" Graham's blunt response: "No." Then he explained: "In effect that would mean that the stock market experts as a whole could beat themselves—a logical contradiction."[1]

~

"I see no reason why they [investors] should be content with results inferior to those of an indexed fund."

---

[1] There is no evidence that professional experts earn higher returns than individual amateurs, nor that any class of institutional investor (e.g., pension managers or mutual fund managers) earns higher returns than any other class.

Then he was asked whether investors should be content with earning the market's return. Graham's answer: "*Yes*." All these years later, the central theme of this *Little Book* is enabling investors to earn their fair share of the stock market's return. *Only* the low-cost traditional index fund can guarantee that outcome.

In the same interview, Benjamin Graham was asked about the objection made to the index fund—that different investors have different requirements. Again, he responded bluntly: "At bottom that is only a convenient cliché or alibi to justify the mediocre record of the past. All investors want good results from their investments, and are entitled to them to the extent that they are actually obtainable. *I see no reason why they should be content with results inferior to those of an indexed fund or pay standard fees for such inferior results.*"

The down-to-earth basics of portfolio policy.

The name Benjamin Graham is intimately connected, indeed almost synonymous, with "value investing" and the search for undervalued securities. But his classic book gives far more attention to the down-to-earth basics of portfolio policy—the straightforward, uncomplicated principles of diversification and rational long-term expectations, also overarching themes of this *Little Book* that you are now reading—than to solving the sphinx-like riddle of selecting superior stocks through careful security analysis.

Finding superior value was once a rewarding activity, but no longer.

Graham was well aware that the superior rewards he had personally reaped by using his valuation principles would be difficult to achieve in the future. In that 1976 interview, he made this remarkable concession, "I am no longer an advocate of elaborate techniques of security analysis in order to find superior value opportunities. This was a rewarding activity, say, 40 years ago, but the situation has changed a great deal since then. In the old days, any well-trained security analyst could do a good professional job of selecting undervalued issues through detailed studies. *But in the light of the enormous amount of research now being carried on, I doubt whether in most cases such extensive efforts will generate sufficiently superior selections to justify their cost.*"

It is fair to say that, by Graham's demanding standards, the overwhelming majority of today's mutual funds, largely because of their high costs and speculative behavior, have failed to live up to their promise. As a result, the traditional index fund has now moved toward ascendancy in investor preferences.

Why? Both because of what it does—providing the broadest possible diversification—and because of what it doesn't do—neither assessing high management fees nor engaging in high portfolio turnover. These paraphrases of Graham's copybook maxims are an important part of his legacy to that vast majority of shareholders who, he believed, should follow the principles he outlined for the defensive investor.

"To achieve satisfactory investment results is easier than most people realize."

It is Benjamin Graham's common sense, intelligence, clear thinking, simplicity, and sense of financial history—along with his willingness to hold fast to the sound principles of long-term investing—that constitute his lasting legacy. He sums up his advice: "Fortunately for the typical investor, it is by no means necessary for his success that he bring the time-honored qualities . . . of courage, knowledge, judgment and experience . . . to bear upon his program—provided he limits his ambition to his capacity and confines his activities within the safe and narrow path of standard, defensive investment. *To achieve satisfactory investment results is easier than most people realize; to achieve superior results is harder than it looks."*

When it's so easy—in fact unbelievably simple—to capture the stock market's returns through an index fund, you don't need to assume extra risks—nor the burden of excessive costs—to earn superior results. With Benjamin Graham's long perspective, common sense, hard realism, and wise intellect, there is no doubt whatsoever in my mind that he would have applauded the index fund. Indeed, as you'll read in Warren Buffett's words that follow, that's precisely what he did.

Don't Take My Word for It

While Benjamin Graham's clearly written commentary can easily be read as an endorsement of a low-cost all-stock-market index fund, don't take my word for it. Listen instead to **Warren Buffett**, his protégé and collaborator whose counsel and practical aid Graham acknowledged as invaluable in the final edition of *The Intelligent Investor*. In 1993, Buffett unequivocally endorsed the index fund. In 2006, he went even further, not only reaffirming this endorsement, but personally assuring me that, decades earlier, Graham himself had endorsed the index fund.

Mr. Buffett spoke these words directly to me at a dinner in Omaha in 2006: "A low-cost index fund is the most sensible equity investment for the great majority of investors. My mentor, Ben Graham, took this position many years ago, and everything I have seen since convinces me of its truth."

* * *

I can only add, after Forrest Gump, "And that's all I have to say about that."

Chapter Eighteen

Asset Allocation I: Stocks and Bonds

~

When You Begin to Invest. As You Accumulate Assets. When You Retire.

IN THIS CHAPTER AND the next, we tackle two complex issues: the general principles of asset allocation, and allocation funds specifically designed for your retirement years. These are issues that have no easy answers.

Why? First, because we investors have a wide range of investment goals, risk tolerances, and behavioral characteristics.

Second, because we've had 35 years of extraordinary returns in the stock market and the bond market alike, returns that are highly unlikely to recur in the coming decade. (See Chapter 9, "When the Good Times No Longer Roll.")

Third, authors of books on investing, are, in a real sense, captives of the eras that we have experienced. For example, when Benjamin Graham wrote *The Intelligent Investor* in 1949, he had *never* experienced a year in which the interest rate on bonds exceeded the dividend yield on stocks. By way of contrast, as I write this chapter in 2017, I have witnessed 60 consecutive years in which the dividend yield on stocks has *never* exceeded the interest rate on bonds. Turnabout, it seems, is fair play.

So instead of looking back and mining the voluminous data on past returns and risks on stocks and bonds, I'll discuss clear principles that you can apply in your current situation. Whether you are accumulating investment assets during your working years or are making withdrawals from your assets in your retirement years, I hope to help you establish appropriate asset allocations for your future.

Ninety-four percent of the differences in portfolio returns is explained by asset allocation.

Benjamin Graham believed that your first investment decision should be how to allocate your investment assets: How much should you hold in stocks? How much in bonds? Graham believed that this strategic decision may well be the most important of your investment lifetime.

A landmark 1986 academic study confirmed his view. The study found that asset allocation accounted for an astonishing 94 percent of the differences in total returns achieved by institutionally managed pension funds.

That 94 percent figure suggests that long-term fund investors might profit by concentrating more on the allocation of their investments between stock funds and bond funds, and less on the question of which particular funds to hold.

— ≈ —

Benjamin Graham's standard division: 50/50.

Where do we begin? Let's start with Benjamin Graham's advice regarding asset allocation in his 1949 classic, *The Intelligent Investor*:

> We have suggested as a fundamental guiding rule that the investor should never have less than 25 percent or more than 75 percent of his funds in common stocks, with a consequent inverse range of between 75 percent and 25 percent in bonds. There is an implication here

that the standard division should be an equal one, or 50–50, between the two major investment mediums.

Furthermore, a truly conservative investor will be satisfied with the gains shown on half his portfolio in a rising market, while in a severe decline he may derive much solace (à la Rochefoucauld[1]) from reflecting how much better off he is than many of his more venturesome friends.

～

Asset allocations and differences in yields.

To today's investors and their advisers, that 50/50 stock/bond allocation—and that range of 75/25 to 25/75—may well seem too conservative. But in 1949, when Graham wrote his book, the yield on stocks was 6.9 percent, and the yield on bonds was 1.9 percent. Today, stock yields are 2.0 percent and bond yields are 3.1 percent—a world of difference in deciding on how much to allocate to stocks and to bonds.[2]

That difference can be measured in two major ways: (1) The gross income yield on a 50/50 stock/bond portfolio has dropped by fully 40 percent, from 4.4 percent to 2.6 percent. (2) The yield tables have been turned upside

---

[1] An apparent reference to the maxim, "We all have strength enough to endure the misfortunes of others."

[2] The bond yield represents a portfolio consisting of one-half corporate bonds (3.9 percent) and one-half U.S. Treasury 10-year notes (2.3 percent).

down, with stocks providing an annual yield *premium* of 5.0 percent in 1949 (amazing!), and a yield *discount* of 1.1 percent in 2017.

When I discussed Graham's philosophy in my 1993 book *Bogle on Mutual Funds: New Perspectives for the Intelligent Investor*, the use of just two asset classes was my starting point. My recommendations for investors in the accumulation phase of their lives, working to build their wealth, focused on a stock/bond mix of 80/20 for younger investors and 70/30 for older investors. For investors starting the postretirement distribution phase, 60/40 for younger investors, 50/50 for older investors.

Bumps along the road.

Despite today's far lower level of interest rates and dividend yields, the great bull market since Graham's era, and the bumps along the way (including the stock market crashes in 1973–1974 and 1987, the bursting of the dot-com bubble in 2000, and the global financial crisis of 2008–2009), the general principles Graham enunciated all those years ago remain remarkably intact. His suggested asset allocation percentages still form a sound starting point for a sensible investment program.

~
Ability to take risk, willingness to take risk.

There are two fundamental factors that determine how you should allocate your portfolio between stocks and bonds: (1) your *ability* to take risk and (2) your *willingness* to take risk.

Your ability to take risk depends on a combination of factors, including your financial position; your future liabilities (for example, retirement income, college tuition for your children and/or grandchildren, a down payment on a home); and how many years you have available to fund those liabilities. In general, you are able to accept more risk if these liabilities are relatively far in the future. Similarly, as you accumulate more assets relative to your liabilities, your ability to take risk increases.

Your willingness to take risk, on the other hand, is purely a matter of preference. Some investors can handle the ups and downs of the market without worry. But if you can't sleep at night because you're frightened about the volatility of your portfolio, you're probably taking more risk than you can handle. Taken together, your ability to accept risk and your willingness to accept risk constitute your *risk tolerance*.

─────────── ∾ ───────────

**A basic allocation model for the investor
who is accumulating assets, and the investor
who is retired.**

Let's begin with a basic allocation model for the accumulation of assets for the wealth-building investor. The main points to consider are merely common sense. (1) Investors seeking to accumulate assets by investing regularly can afford to take somewhat more risk—that is, to be more aggressive—than investors who have a relatively fixed pool of capital and are dependent on income and even distributions from their capital to meet their day-to-day living expenses. (2) Younger investors, with more time to let the magic of compounding work for them, can also afford to be more aggressive, while older investors will likely want to steer a more conservative course.

Graham's allocation guidelines are reasonable; mine are similar but more flexible. Your common stock position should be as large as your tolerance to take risk permits. For example, my highest recommended general target allocation for stocks would be 80 percent for younger investors accumulating assets over a long time frame.

My lowest target stock allocation, 25 percent, would apply to older investors late in their retirement years. These investors must give greater weight to the short-run *consequences* of their actions than to the *probabilities* of future returns. They must recognize that volatility of returns is an imperfect measure of risk. Far more meaningful is the risk that they will unexpectedly have to liquidate assets when cash is needed to meet living expenses—often in depressed markets—and perhaps receive less in proceeds than the original cost of the assets. In investing, there are no guarantees.

Four decisions.

As an intelligent investor, you must make four decisions about your asset allocation program:

- First, and most important, you must make a strategic choice in allocating your assets between stocks and bonds. Differently situated investors with unique needs and circumstances will obviously make different decisions.
- Second, the decision to maintain either a fixed ratio or a ratio that varies with market returns cannot be sidestepped. The fixed ratio (periodically rebalancing to the original asset allocation) is a prudent

choice that limits risk and may well be the better choice for most investors. The portfolio that
is never rebalanced, however, is likely to provide
higher long-term returns.

- Third is the decision as to whether to introduce an
  element of tactical allocation, varying the stock/bond
  ratio as market conditions change. Tactical allocation carries its own risks. Changes in the stock/bond
  ratio may add value, but (more likely, I think) they
  may not. In our uncertain world, tactical changes
  should be made sparingly, for they imply a certain
  prescience that few, if any, of us possess. In general,
  investors should not engage in tactical allocation.

- Fourth, and perhaps most important, is the decision
  as to whether to focus on actively managed mutual
  funds or traditional index funds. Clear and convincing evidence points to the index fund strategy.

All four of these decisions require tough, demanding
choices by the intelligent investor. With thoughtfulness,
care, and prudence, you can make these choices sensibly.

—— ～ ——

**The link between risk premiums and cost
penalties.**

Yes, the allocation of your investment portfolio between stocks and bonds will likely be an important determinant of your wealth accumulation. But too few investors are aware of the critical linkage between fund costs and asset allocation.

A low-cost portfolio with a *lower* allocation to stocks (and therefore *lower* risk) can earn the same or even a *higher* net return than a portfolio with a far higher allocation to stocks (and therefore *higher* risk); provided only that the costs of investing in the lower-risk alternative are materially below those in the higher-risk alternative.

Perhaps this simple example will help (Exhibit 18.1). Here, we assume that one investor holds a 75/25 stock/ bond portfolio with expected gross annual returns of 6 percent on stocks and 3 percent on bonds. The investor in actively managed funds incurs all-in costs, respectively,

EXHIBIT 18.1 By Reducing Costs, You Can Earn Higher Return with Lower Risk

High-Cost Actively Managed Funds				Low-Cost Index Funds			
	Stocks	Bonds	Portfolio Impact		Stocks	Bonds	Portfolio Impact
Allocation	75%	25%	–	Allocation	25%	75%	–
Gross return	6	3	5.25%	Gross return	6	3	3.75%
Costs	2	1	1.75	Costs	0.05	0.10	0.09
Net return	4.0%	2.0%	3.50%	Net return	6.0%	2.9%	3.66%

of 2 percent and 1 percent annually. The expected net return on that portfolio would be 3.5 percent.

Holding those returns on stocks and bonds constant, now assume that a much more conservative investor holds a 25/75 portfolio—precisely the reverse allocation. But the investor replaces those high-cost actively managed mutual funds with low-cost index funds charging 0.05 percent for stocks and 0.10 percent for bonds. With that balanced index portfolio, the expected net return on the portfolio would actually increase, to 3.66 percent annually.

Low costs enable lower-risk portfolios to provide higher returns than higher-risk portfolios.

In this example, simply by taking the drag of excessive costs out of the equation, the 25/75 stock/bond portfolio would outpace the 75/25 portfolio. *The index fund changes the conventional wisdom about asset allocation.*

Cost matters! Risk premium and cost penalty, ever at war with each other, must find their way into the process of balancing the stocks and bonds in your portfolio. It's about time.

Let me be clear: I am not suggesting that you should slash your equity allocation if you replace your high-cost actively managed funds with low-cost index funds. But I am suggesting that if you hold actively managed stock and bond funds in your asset allocation, with fees far higher than those of low-cost index funds, you should consider what is likely to produce the best net return. Just do the simple math.

———————— ∽ ————————

A human perspective: advice to a worried investor.

There is little science to establishing a precise asset allocation strategy. But we could do worse than beginning with Ben Graham's central target of a 50/50 stock/bond balance, with a range limited to 75/25 and 25/75, divided between plain-vanilla stock and bond index funds.

But allocations need not be precise. They are also about judgment, hope, fear, and risk tolerance. No bullet-proof strategy is available to investors. Even I worry about the allocation of my own portfolio.

In the letter that follows, I explain my concerns to a young investor worried about possible future catastrophes in our fragile world and in our changing society, as he tries to determine a sensible asset allocation for his own portfolio.

> I believe that the U.S. economy will continue to grow over the long term, and that the intrinsic value of the stock market will reflect that growth. Why? Because that intrinsic value is created by dividend yields and earnings growth, which historically have had a correlation of

about 0.96 with our nation's economic growth as measured by GDP. (Close to 1.00, a perfect correlation.)

Of course there will be times when stock market prices rise above (or fall below) that intrinsic value. This may well be a time when some overvaluation exists. (Or not. We can never be sure.) But in the long run, market prices have always, finally, converged on intrinsic value. I believe (with Warren Buffett) that's just the way things are, totally rational.

Substantial risks—some known, some unknown— of course exist. You and I know as much—or as little— about their happening as anyone else. We're on our own in assessing the probabilities as well as the consequences. But if we don't invest, we end up with nothing.

My own total portfolio holds about 50/50 indexed stocks and bonds, largely indexed short- and intermediate-term. At my age of 88, I'm comfortable with that allocation. But I confess that half of the time I worry that I have too much in equities, and the other half of the time that I don't have enough in equities. Finally, we're all just human beings, operating in a fog of ignorance and relying on our circumstances and our common sense to establish an appropriate asset allocation.

Paraphrasing Churchill on democracy, "my investment strategy is the worst strategy ever devised ... except for every other strategy that has been tried." I hope these comments help. Good luck.

J.C.B.

And good luck to the readers of this chapter. Do your best, for there are no easy answers to the challenge of asset allocation.

Chapter Nineteen

Asset Allocation II

~

*Retirement Investing, and Funds That Set
Your Asset Allocation in Advance.*

IN MY 1993 BOOK *Bogle on Mutual Funds*, after discussing the large number of asset allocation strategies available to investors, I raised the possibility that "less is more"—that a simple mainstream (i.e., index) balanced fund, 60 percent in U.S. stocks, 40 percent in U.S. bonds, one that provides extraordinary diversification and operates at rock-bottom cost, would offer the functional equivalent of having your entire portfolio overseen by an investment advisory firm.

It was in 1992 that I decided to form just such a 60/40 stock/bond balanced index fund at Vanguard. Viewed through the lens of the quarter-century that followed, the fund has been an extraordinary success (Exhibit 19.1).

Let's look at the remarkable record of that balanced index fund. During its 25-year lifetime, the fund has earned an annual return of 8.0 percent, as compared to 6.3 percent for its peers, an advantage of 1.7 percentage points per year. That margin resulted in a compound advantage in cumulative return of 202 percentage points.

The balanced index fund's advantage has largely been the result of its low costs—an expense ratio of 0.14 percent versus 1.34 percent for its balanced mutual fund peer group. That expense ratio advantage and the remarkable 0.98 correlation of its annual returns with those of its peers (1.00 is perfect correlation) give us every reason to

EXHIBIT 19.1 **The Low-Cost Balanced Index Portfolio versus Its High-Cost Peers, 1992–2016**

| | Returns | | Expense Ratio |
	Annual*	Cumulative	
Balanced index fund	8.0%	+536%	0.14%
Average balanced mutual fund	6.3	334	1.34
Index advantage	1.7%	+202%	1.20%

*Correlation of annual returns, 0.98.

expect the balanced index fund to outperform its peers in the years ahead.

Yes, an investor would have been better off by holding a low-cost S&P 500 Index fund, with an annual return of 9.3 percent during this period versus the balanced index fund's return of 8.1 percent. With its lower volatility (balanced index 8.9 percent, 500 index 14.3 percent), its advantage in risk-adjusted return would be even higher. But when there was trouble, the balanced index fund offered exceptional protection. During 2000–2002, when the S&P 500 declined by 38 percent, the balanced index fund fell just 14 percent. In 2008, with the S&P 500 off 37 percent, the fund was off just 22 percent.

For investors who have a very long time horizon, and considerable grit and guts—investors who have the courage to be unintimidated by periodic market crashes—clearly an allocation of 100 percent to the S&P 500 Index fund would nearly always be the better choice. (Its margin was unusually close over the past 25 years; I expect the spread to be wider going forward.)

But what if you have a limited time horizon, or are cowed by stock market volatility and tempted to liquidate your stock portion when the seas are rough? Then the hands-off, set-the-allocation-and-stay-the-course strategy of the fixed 60/40 stock/bond asset allocation of the balanced index fund represents an option worthy of your serious consideration.

---------------------------- ∿ ----------------------------

The wisdom of Benjamin Graham, again.

I see no reason for the retired investor to depart far from the advice that Benjamin Graham offered to all investors those many years ago, as reported in the previous chapter—a basic allocation of 50 percent stocks and 50 percent bonds, with a range of between 75/25 and 25/75. The higher equity portion for more risk-tolerant investors, perhaps seeking greater wealth for themselves and their heirs; the lower ratio for risk-averse investors, willing to sacrifice the potential for greater returns for some extra peace of mind.

I've often been cited as an advocate for a similar simple and seemingly rigid asset allocation: your bond position should equal your age, with the remainder in stocks. That asset allocation strategy can serve the needs of many—if not most—investors quite well, but it was never intended to be more than a rule of thumb, a place to begin your thought process. It is (or was!) based on the idea that when we are younger, have limited assets to invest, don't need investment income, have a higher tolerance for risk, and believe that equities will provide higher returns than bonds over the long term, we should own more stocks than bonds.

But when we grow older and ultimately retire, most of us will have accumulated a significant investment portfolio. Then, we are apt to be more risk averse, more willing to sacrifice maximum capital appreciation and to rely more heavily on the higher income yields that bonds have provided over the past 60 years. Under these circumstances, we should own more bonds than stocks.

─────────────── ∼ ───────────────

The need for flexibility.

I hardly intended such an age-based rule of thumb to be rigidly applied. For example, surely many young investors beginning their first full-time jobs might as well regularly invest not 75 percent, but 100 percent of their savings in equities during those early years of investing.

And zero percent in equities is likely a dubious goal for a new centenarian. (We will have lots more centenarians as time goes on.) Continually selling equities by such an investor to reduce the stock allocation might not make much sense, especially if you consider the potential for large taxes on capital gains that are realized when stocks with substantial appreciation are sold.

A flexible age-based plan comports with our common sense. But the many studies that have been done to validate the wide variety of similar (but more precise and more complex) allocation strategies have a common flaw: they are based on past returns on bonds and on stocks, neither of which seem likely to be repeated in the coming decade. (See Chapter 9.)

"The checks are in the mail."

Which brings me to an even more important point. As we age, we begin to rely less on the human capital that has largely got us to where we are today, and more on our investment capital. Finally, what's most important when we retire is the stream of income we need to support our needs—the dividend checks we receive from our mutual fund investments and the monthly checks we receive from our Social Security payments.

Yes, the market value of our capital is important. But frequent peeking at the value of our investments is not only unproductive, but counterproductive. What we really seek is retirement income that is steady and, if possible, grows with inflation.

Social Security fits those criteria perfectly. And, with moderate risk, a balanced mutual fund portfolio can effectively supplement (or be supplemented by) Social

Security payments. About half of the balanced portfolio's income comes from interest on bonds, and the other half from dividends, mostly from large-cap stocks. With only three significant exceptions, the dividends on the S&P 500 Index have increased every year since the Index began 90 years ago, in 1926. (See Exhibit 6.2 in Chapter 6.)

Social Security payments plus index fund dividends—a sound basis for steady and growing income.

A combination of Social Security payments and dividends from index funds[1] (supplemented as necessary with withdrawals of capital) are likely to be an effective means of enjoying regular monthly income from your retirement assets. (Although few equity mutual funds pay dividends monthly, most have programs for providing regularly scheduled monthly payments.)

The income yields on stocks and bonds are near historical lows (stocks 2 percent, bonds 3 percent), and because of the pernicious impact of mutual fund expenses,

---

[1] As shown in Exhibit 6.3 in Chapter 6, actively managed funds confiscate most—if not all—of the gross dividend income they earn. The index fund does not.

the yields on actively managed mutual funds are much lower, as we saw in Chapter 6. Such low yields are unlikely to adequately satisfy the retirement income needs of many investors. So investors will be better served to consider generating retirement income through a total return approach—using a combination of fund dividends and regular withdrawals from accumulated capital to generate a steady stream of monthly checks during retirement.

Non-U.S. stocks—a new paradigm for allocation?

During the past decade, acceptance of the traditional *two-fund* model portfolio (U.S. bonds and stocks) has largely been superseded by a *three-fund* model portfolio: 33 percent in a bond index fund, 33 percent in a U.S. stock index fund, and 33 percent in a non-U.S. stock index fund.

Such a three-fund portfolio allocation simply reflects the broad acceptance of a global portfolio by many advisers and investors. Such a portfolio is essentially based on the market capitalizations of the stocks of nearly all of the world's nations.

In my 1993 book *Bogle on Mutual Funds*, I advised investors that they did not need to hold non-U.S. stocks in their portfolios, and in any event should not allocate more than 20 percent of their stock portion to non-U.S. stocks.

My view that a U.S.-only equity portfolio will serve the needs of most investors was (and still is) challenged by, well, everyone. As the argument goes, "Isn't omitting non-U.S. stocks from a diversified portfolio just as arbitrary as, say, omitting the technology sector from the S&P 500?"

I argued the contra side. We Americans earn our money in dollars, spend it in dollars, save it in dollars, and invest it in dollars, so why take currency risk? Haven't U.S. institutions been generally stronger than those of other nations? Don't half of the revenues and profits of U.S. corporations already come from outside the United States? Isn't U.S. gross domestic product (GDP) likely to grow at least as fast as the GDP of the rest of the developed world, perhaps at an even higher rate?

———————— ∾ ————————

The advice in my 1993 book has worked out well.

For whatever reason, my advice has worked out well. Since 1993, the U.S. S&P 500 Index has earned an average annual return of 9.4 percent (cumulative +707 percent). The non-U.S. portfolio—I refer here to the MSCI Europe, Australasia, and Far East Index (EAFE)—has had an annual return of 5.1 percent (+216 percent).

That said, perhaps the relative advantage achieved in the U.S. stock market over the past quarter-century has now been arbitraged away, and that long period of relative underperformance by non-U.S. stocks has led to more attractive valuations abroad. Who really knows? So you will have to consider the probabilities and make your own judgment.

———————————— ∽ ————————————

A fixed stock/bond ratio? Or a ratio that changes with investor goals, or with time?

The goal of the balanced index fund with a fixed stock/bond ratio was to relieve investors of the challenges of allocating assets as markets change. But I soon came to the (obvious!) conclusion that the arbitrary 60/40 balanced portfolio—perhaps the most sensible ratio for investors seeking to balance risk and return—might not be suitable for all investors. So why not offer funds with other allocations?

So in 1994, Vanguard began to offer four "LifeStrategy" Funds (Exhibit 19.2)—Growth (80 percent equities), Moderate Growth (60 percent), Conservative Growth (40 percent), and Income (20 percent). Each of these equity allocations now include 60 percent U.S. stocks and

EXHIBIT 19.2 Asset Allocations of Various Balanced Funds

	Balanced Index	LifeStrategy Growth	LifeStrategy Moderate Growth	LifeStrategy Conservative Growth	LifeStrategy Income	Target Retirement 2060	Target Retirement 2055	Target Retirement 2050
U.S. stocks	60%	48%	36%	24%	12%	54%	54%	54%
Non-U.S. stocks	0	32	24	16	8	36	36	36
Stocks total	60%	80%	60%	40%	20%	90%	90%	90%
U.S. bonds	40%	14%	28%	42%	56%	7%	7%	7%
Non-U.S. bonds	0	6	12	18	24	3	3	3
Bonds total	40%	20%	40%	60%	80%	10%	10%	10%

	Target Retirement 2045	Target Retirement 2040	Target Retirement 2035	Target Retirement 2030	Target Retirement 2025	Target Retirement 2020	Target Retirement 2015	Target Retirement Income
U.S. stocks	54%	52%	48%	43%	39%	34%	27%	18%
Non-U.S. stocks	36	35	32	29	26	23	18	12
Stocks total	90%	87%	80%	72%	65%	56%	44%	30%
U.S. bonds	7%	9%	15%	20%	25%	32%	42%	54%
Non-U.S. bonds	3	4	6	8	11	12	14	16
Bonds total	10%	13%	21%	28%	35%	44%	56%	70%

40 percent non-U.S. stocks; each bond allocation includes 70 percent U.S. bonds and 30 percent non-U.S. bonds).

The rise of the target-date fund (TDF).

The LifeStrategy funds are by no means the only variation in the balanced fund concept. Over the past decade, there has been an explosion in investor demand for target-date funds (TDFs)—funds that hold diversified portfolios of stocks and bonds that gradually become more conservative as the fund approaches its target date, usually the year that the investor expects to retire.

Target-date funds for retirement are by far the most popular, now holding assets of nearly $1 trillion. And their concept—essentially, replacing stocks with bonds as the need to fund future liabilities draws closer—can be applied to other investment goals as well, such as children's college expenses. One of the reasons for the popularity of target-date funds is their simplicity. All you need to do is estimate what year you plan to retire or your child will start college, and then invest in the fund closest to that target date. "Set it and forget it" is the idea.

TDFs can be an excellent choice, not only for investors who are just getting started with their investment programs, but also for investors who decide to adopt a simple strategy for funding their retirement. But as your assets accumulate and your personal balance sheet and investment goals become more complicated, it is worth considering the use of individual building blocks like low-cost stock and bond index funds to construct your portfolio.

If you choose to invest in TDFs, I encourage you to "look under the hood" first. (Always a good idea!) Compare the costs of TDFs, and pay attention to their underlying structures. Many TDFs hold actively managed funds as components, whereas others use low-cost index funds.

Make sure you know precisely what is in your TDF portfolio and how much you're paying for it. The major actively managed TDFs have annual expense ratios that average 0.70 percent; index fund TDFs carry average expense ratios of 0.13 percent. It will not surprise you to know that I believe that low-cost, index-based target-date funds are likely to be your best option.

Don't forget Social Security.

Whatever asset allocation strategy you decide is best for you, you absolutely must take into account the role of Social Security—a major source of income for most retirees—as you age. In fact, some 93 percent of retired Americans collect Social Security. When determining their asset allocations, most investors need to take Social Security into consideration as a bond-like asset.

The value of Social Security in your portfolio is significant. I'll illustrate this with an example. The average remaining life expectancy for a 62-year-old American is about 20 years, so I'll assume that at age 62, an investor will collect Social Security for 20 years. With a final salary of $60,000, an investor who claims Social Security right away would receive $1,174 per month. If we discount that benefit by the current rate on inflation-adjusted Treasury bonds, the investor's Social Security would have a capitalized value of about $270,000. But since that value vanishes on the death of the retiree, let's arbitrarily discount it by about one-fourth, to a revised value of $200,000. (Later, I'll come back to the topic of *when* to claim Social Security.)

Now let's assume our investor has a portfolio of mutual funds worth $1 million and uses Benjamin Graham's classic 50/50 allocation. Ignoring Social Security, the investor would allocate $500,000 each into stocks and bonds. But we shouldn't ignore Social Security.

~

Social Security and asset allocation.

When we add the $200,000 imputed value of Social Security to the investor's portfolio, it would total $1,200,000. But with that extra Social Security investment, the bond-like portion of the portfolio rises to $700,000 or 58 percent, with 42 percent in stocks.

To achieve a true 50/50 allocation, the investor would allocate $600,000 in stocks and $600,000 in bonds ($400,000 in bond mutual funds, $200,000 in Social Security). Target-date funds generally ignore Social Security income, which leads to investors holding more conservative portfolios than they might realize. While TDFs may ignore Social Security as a bond-like asset, you should not.

Caution: Deferring Social Security payments substantially enhances the monthly payments you later receive, but at the expense of not receiving any Social Security payments at all during the interim years. Investors must balance the opportunity to increase their eventual monthly payments against the absence of those monthly payments over a full decade.

For example, our investor with annual earnings of $60,000 would receive about $1,174 per month if payments began at age 62. By deferring Social Security until age 72, the monthly payments would increase to $1,974—a remarkable increase of almost 70 percent. But by deferring payments for 10 years, that investor would have missed out on a total of $140,900 in Social

Security payments. It would take 14 years of collecting the higher monthly benefits to break even on those deferred payments.

Retirement Accounts

Accumulating wealth for a secure and comfortable retirement is the primary investment goal for many—if not most—investors. Tax-advantaged retirement savings vehicles make achieving that goal much easier. While you should be sure to take advantage of these retirement accounts, you must decide which one (or which combination) is right for you. Here's a brief overview of the various types of retirement savings accounts available in the United States:

Defined contribution (DC) plans are offered by many employers, and the plans allow you, the employee/investor, to defer income directly out of your pay and into your retirement account. The most common DC plan is the 401(k), which allows you to save money for retirement on a pretax basis, and your contributions are often matched by your employer according to a predetermined formula. Investment returns on your assets grow on a tax-deferred basis until you withdraw them in retirement.

There are often provisions for loans from your account or early withdrawals in case you experience financial hardship during your working years. Similar plans exist for employees of other types of organizations: the 403(b) plan for nonprofit corporations, the 457 plan for certain nonprofits and state and municipal government employees, and the Thrift Savings Plan (TSP) for federal government employees.

Traditional IRAs can be set up by any wage earner. The tax advantages of the traditional IRA are similar to those of the DC plan—your contributions are usually tax-deductible, and grow tax-deferred until you withdraw them. Maximum annual contribution is usually $5,500.

SEP IRAs: The Simplified Employee Pension IRA is designed for self-employed individuals and small-business owners. The tax treatment is similar to that for traditional IRAs, but the maximum contribution limits are much higher.

Roth IRAs: The Roth IRA has a different tax treatment than the other retirement accounts. There is no tax deduction for your

(continued)

contributions (they are fully taxed), but withdrawals upon retirement are entirely tax-free—including any accumulated gains on your assets. Unlike DC plans and IRAs, the accumulations on your Roth account are never taxed. Roth contributions can be made to many DC plans as well.

The Roth IRA is likely the better choice for most new investors, but investors in existing traditional IRAs should be aware that converting to a Roth IRA likely entails taxes on the transfer that may be substantial. Do the math!

—————————— ≈ ——————————

The need to draw down capital.

With the current interest rate on bonds at roughly 3 percent and the dividend yield on stocks at 2 percent (in both cases, before the high costs of actively managed funds), the income produced by your retirement portfolio is apt to fall well short of your retirement spending needs. A rule of thumb suggests that an annual withdrawal rate of 4 percent (including income and capital) of the year-end value of your initial retirement capital, adjusted annually for inflation, is likely—but by no means guaranteed—to be sustainable throughout your retirement years.

Do not adhere rigorously to spending rules such as 4 percent annually. Maintain a level of flexibility in your retirement spending plan. If the markets are particularly bad and your spending rule would take too large a bite out of your portfolio, tighten your belt and draw down a little less. If the markets are good and your spending rate provides larger payments than you need, reinvest the unexpected windfall for the ever-uncertain future. By so doing, you'll reduce spending from the portfolio when the markets are depressed and have the opportunity to recoup your capital when the markets recover.

No guarantees.

Let me reiterate: Any asset allocation strategy is subject to numerous risks—stock market risk, payout risk, macroeconomic risk, and other risks in the fragile world in which we exist. All we can do is make informed judgments, and then be flexible in our allocation and payouts as conditions change.

Don't Take My Word for It

With all of the more sophisticated allocation options now available, the merits of the simple 60/40 stock/bond balanced index fund are often ignored. But early in 2017, **Ben Carlson**, author of *A Wealth of Common Sense*, saluted the concept in "A Lesson in Investing Simplicity: Why the Bogle Model Beats the Yale Model," an article reprinted in *MarketWatch*.

"Every year, the NACUBO-Commonfund Study of Endowments" reports the investment returns achieved by "more than 800 college endowments, representing $515 billion in assets."

Mr. Carlson uses what he calls "the Bogle Model," a portfolio of 40 percent Total (U.S.) Stock Market Index Fund, 20 percent Total International Stock Index Fund, and 40 percent Total (U.S.) Bond Market Index Fund. The table shows how the Bogle model has outperformed the average university endowments consistently in significant time periods ending June 30, 2016. For the full decade, the model has even outpaced the top-decile endowment funds.

Mr. Carlson concludes, "This has nothing to do with active vs. passive investing. This is all

The Bogle Model Outperforms the Top University Endowments Returns through June 30, 2016

	The Bogle Model	Average Endowment	Top-Quartile Endowment	Top-Decile Endowment
3 Years	6.4%	5.2%	6.3%	6.6%
5 Years	6.5	5.4	6.2	6.6
10 Years	6.0	5.0	5.3	5.4

Source: NACUBO-Commonfund Study of Endowments.

about simple vs. complex, operationally efficient investment programs vs. operationally inefficient investment programs, and high-probability portfolios vs. low-probability portfolios. Investing is hard enough as it is before introducing a complex, inefficient, low-probability investment style. That's why the simple, efficient, high-probability Bogle Model wins."

* * *

NOTE: The 60/40 Balanced Index Fund, holding only U.S. stocks in its equity allocation, earned significantly higher returns than the "Bogle Model": 3 years 8.4 percent; 5 years 8.6 percent; 10 years 6.9 percent. Only time will tell which of these two strategies will be superior in the years ahead.

Chapter Twenty

Investment Advice That Meets the Test of Time

Channeling Benjamin Franklin

DEEP DOWN, I REMAIN absolutely confident that the vast majority of American families would be well served by owning their equity holdings in a Standard & Poor's 500 Index fund (or a total stock market index fund) and holding their bonds in a total bond market index fund. (Investors in high tax brackets, however, would instead own a very low-cost quasi-index portfolio of high-grade intermediate-term municipal bonds.) To repeat, *while such an index-driven strategy may not be the best investment strategy ever devised, the number of investment strategies that are worse is infinite.*

Hear Warren Buffett: "*Most investors, both institutional and individual, will find that the best way to own common stocks is through an index fund that charges minimal fees. Those following this path are sure to beat the net results (after fees and expenses) delivered by the great majority of investment professionals.*" (Don't forget that an index fund with minimal fees is also, for most investors, the best way to own bonds.)

For all of the inevitable uncertainty amid the eternally dense fog surrounding the world of investing, there remains much that we do know.

As you seek investment success, realize that we can never know what returns stocks and bonds will deliver in the years ahead, nor the future returns that might be achieved by alternatives to the index portfolio. But take heart. For all the inevitable uncertainty amid the eternally dense fog surrounding the world of investing, there remains much that we do know. Just consider these commonsense realities:

- We *know* that we must start to invest at the earliest possible moment, and continue to put money away regularly from then on.

- We *know* that investing entails risk. But we also know that not investing dooms us to financial failure.

- We *know* the sources of returns in the stock and bond markets, and that's the beginning of wisdom.

- We *know* that the risk of selecting individual securities, as well as the risk of selecting both fund managers and investment styles, can be eliminated by the total diversification offered by the traditional index fund. Only market risk remains.

- We *know* that costs matter, overpoweringly in the long run, and we know that we must minimize them.

- We *know* that taxes matter, and that they, too, must be minimized.

- We *know* that neither beating the market nor successfully timing the market can be generalized without self-contradiction. *What may work for the few cannot work for the many.*

- Finally, we *know* what we *don't* know. We can never be certain how our world will look tomorrow, and we know far less about how it will look a decade hence. But with intelligent asset allocation and sensible investment choices, we can be prepared for the inevitable bumps along the road, and should glide right through them.

Our task remains: earning our fair share of whatever returns our business enterprises are generous enough to provide in the years to come. That, to me, is the definition of investment success.

The traditional index fund is the only investment that guarantees the achievement of that goal. Don't count yourself among the losers whose investment returns will fall well short of the returns realized in the stock market. You will be a winner if you follow the simple common-sense guidelines in this *Little Book*.

John Bogle and Benjamin Franklin: parallel investment principles.

As I consider my investment ideas in the context of those I have observed over the long sweep of history, I find, in retrospect, a remarkable set of parallel principles that reflect the wisdom of Benjamin Franklin. Consider this collection of his sayings and mine.

On saving for the future:

Franklin: If you would be wealthy, think of Saving as well as Getting. Remember that time is money. Lost time is never found again.

Bogle: Not investing is a surefire way to fail to accumulate the wealth necessary to ensure a sound financial future. Compound interest is a miracle. Time is your friend. Give yourself all the time that you possibly can.

On the importance of cost control:

Franklin: Beware of little Expenses; a small Leak will sink a great Ship.

Bogle: Basic arithmetic works. Your net return is simply the gross return of your investment portfolio less the costs you incur. So minimize your investment expenses.

On taking risks:

Franklin: There are no Gains, without Pains. He that would catch Fish, must venture his Bait.

Bogle: Invest you must. The biggest risk is the long-term risk of not putting your money to work at a generous return, not the short-term (but nonetheless real) risk of market volatility.

On understanding what's important:

Franklin: An investment in knowledge always pays the best interest. Learning is to the Studious, and Riches to the Careful. If a man empties his purse into his head, no man can take it away from him.

Bogle: To be a successful investor, you need information. If information about past returns earned by mutual funds—especially short-term returns—is close to meaningless, information about risks and costs is priceless.

On the markets:

Franklin: One man may be more cunning than another, but not more cunning than everybody else.

Bogle: Don't think that you know more than the market; no one does. And don't act on insights that you think are your own but are usually shared by millions of others.

On safety:

Franklin: Great Estates may venture more, but little Boats should keep near shore.

Bogle: Whether your assets are great or humble, diversify, diversify, diversify in a portfolio of stocks and bonds. Then, only market risk remains. Investors of modest means should be especially cautious.

On forecasting:

Franklin: 'Tis easy to see, hard to foresee.

Bogle: It takes wisdom to know what we don't know.

On looking after your own interests:

Franklin: If you would have a faithful Servant, serve yourself.

Bogle: You must never ignore your own economic interests.

And finally, on steadfastness:

Franklin: Industry, Perseverance, and Frugality make Fortune yield.

Bogle: No matter what happens, stick to your program. Think long term. Patience and consistency are the most valuable assets for the intelligent investor. "Stay the course."

Yes, I freely concede that eighteenth-century Franklin had a far better way with words than twenty-first-century Bogle. But our near-parallel maxims suggest that the principles of sensible saving and investing are time-tested, perhaps even eternal.

The way to wealth.

The way to wealth, I repeat one final time, is not only to capitalize on the magic of long-term compounding of returns, but to avoid the tyranny of long-term compounding of costs. Avoid the high-cost, high-turnover, opportunistic marketing modalities that characterize today's financial services system. While the interests of Wall Street's *businesses* are well served by the aphorism "Don't just stand there—do something!," the interests of Main Street's *investors* are well served by an approach that is its diametrical opposite: "Don't do something—just stand there!"

Don't Take My Word for It

The ideas in this closing chapter seem like common sense to me, and perhaps they seem like common sense to you as well. But if you have any doubt, listen to their echo in these words by **Clifford S. Asness**, managing principal of AQR Capital Management. "We basically know how to invest. A good analogy is to dieting and diet books. We all know how to lose weight and get in better shape: Eat less and exercise more . . . that is *simple*—but it is not *easy*. Investing is no different.

"Some simple, but not easy, advice for good investing and financial planning in general includes: diversify widely . . . keep costs low . . . rebalance in a disciplined fashion ... spend less ... save more ... make less heroic assumptions about future returns ... when something sounds like a free lunch, assume it is not free unless very convincing arguments are made—and then check again.

"Stop watching the stock markets ... work less on investing, not more. ... In true Hippocratic fashion: Do No Harm! You do not need a magic bullet. Little can change the fact that current expected returns on a broad set of asset classes are low versus history. *Stick to the basics with discipline.*"

* * *

The simple ideas in this book really work. I believe the classic index fund must be the core of such a winning strategy. But even I would not have had the temerity to say what the late **Dr. Paul Samuelson** of MIT said in a speech to the Boston Society of Security Analysts in the autumn of 2005: "*The creation of the first index fund by John Bogle was the equivalent of the invention of the wheel, the alphabet, and wine and cheese.*" Those essentials of our existence that we have come to take for granted have stood the test of time. So will the traditional index fund.

Acknowledgments

IN WRITING THIS BOOK, I have received incredibly wonderful support from the entire (three-person) staff of the Bogle Financial Markets Research Center, the Vanguard-supported unit that began its formal activities at the beginning of 2000.

I'll begin with special thanks to Michael W. Nolan Jr., senior investment analyst and researcher, my partner, and sometimes my conscience. Mike has ably served at my side for six years now, part of his 16-year Vanguard career. Mike has done just about everything but actually write this book—researching subjects, developing data, checking sources, helping to edit the text, and working with the publisher. He has done it not only with excellence but with an equanimity and sense of humor that have to be seen to be believed.

Emily Snyder, my executive assistant for 27 years now (and with 32 years of service on the Vanguard crew), has carried much of the burden of putting my scrawled notes together into a beautifully rendered typescript, and done so with extraordinary skill, steadfast finesse, and unfailing good humor. While I think she winced when I told her that, yes, I'd be writing my eleventh book, she patiently carried me through the usual eight or so edits that I can't help myself from doing—all in the pursuit of a clear, accurate, logical, and reader-friendly text.

Kathy Younker is new to our little group, but she did her share of endless typing and retyping, adjusting the rhythm of my writing to the frantic pace of our activity, also with remarkable skill, patience, and good humor.

I should note that I take full responsibility for the strong opinions expressed in this *Little Book*. These opinions do not necessarily represent the opinions of the present management of Vanguard.

I remain deeply dedicated to Vanguard and our crew members, and continue to "press on, regardless" in the furtherance of the values that I invested in the firm when I founded it in 1974, and during the 25 years in which I served as chief executive, then chairman, and then senior chairman.

JOHN C. BOGLE